An Assessment of Driver Drowsiness, Distraction, and Performance in a Naturalistic Setting

U.S. Department of Transportation

Federal Motor Carrier Safety Administration

February 2011

Technical Report Documentation Page

1. Report No. **FMCSA-RRR-11-010**	2. Government Accession No.	3. Recipient's Catalog No.
4. Title and Subtitle: **An Assessment of Driver Drowsiness, Distraction, and Performance in a Naturalistic Setting**		5. Report Date: **February 2011**
		6. Performing Organization Code
7. Author(s): **Lawrence C. Barr, C. Y. David Yang, Richard J. Hanowski*, and Rebecca Olson***		8. Performing Organization Report No. **DOT-VNTSC-FMCSA-04-01**
9. Performing Organization Name and Address: **U.S. Department of Transportation** **Research and Special Programs Administration** **John A. Volpe National Transportation Systems Center** **Cambridge, MA 02142** ***Virginia Tech Transportation Institute**		10. Work Unit No. (TRAIS)
		11. Contract or Grant No. **SA-1J/AB136**
12. Sponsoring Agency Name and Address: **U.S. Department of Transportation** **Federal Motor Carrier Safety Administration** **1200 New Jersey Ave., SE** **Washington, DC 20590**		13. Type of Report and period covered. **Final Report November 2002– February 2004**
		14. Sponsoring Agency Code
15. Supplementary Notes: **Robert J. Carroll was the FMCSA COTR for this project.**		

16. Abstract:

This report documents the results of a study to characterize episodes of driver drowsiness and to assess the impact of drowsiness on driving performance. This data mining effort performed additional analyses on the data collected in an earlier FMCSA study of the effects of fatigue on drivers in local/short haul operations. The primary objectives of the study were to investigate drowsiness as a naturally occurring phenomenon by identifying and characterizing episodes of drowsiness that occurred during every period of driving and to determine the operational or driving-environment factors associated with drowsy driving. A total of 2,745 drowsy events were identified in approximately 900 total hours of naturalistic driving video data. Higher levels of drowsiness were found to be associated with younger and less experienced drivers. In addition, a strong and consistent relationship was found between drowsiness and time of day. Drowsy driving events were twice as likely to occur between 6 a m. and 9 a m., as compared to baseline, or non-drowsy driving, and approximately 30 percent of all observed instances of drowsiness occurred within the first hour of the work shift. Some interesting insights about the relationship between driver fatigue or drowsiness and driver distraction and inattention are provided. This study presents an analytical framework for quantitatively assessing driver fatigue and drowsiness as a function of driver characteristics and the driving environment.

17. Key Words: **CMV, commercial motor vehicle, driver, drowsiness, fatigue, local/short-haul truck operations, naturalistic driving, performance, statistical models,**		18. Distribution Statement **No restrictions.**	
19. Security Classif. (of this report) **Unclassified**	20. Security Classif. (of this page) **Unclassified**	21. No. of Pages: **92**	22. Price

Form DOT F 1700.7 (8-72)   Reproduction of completed page authorized

FOREWORD

The purpose of this report is to document the results of a study undertaken to characterize episodes of driver fatigue and drowsiness and to assess the impact of driver fatigue on driving performance. This data mining effort performed additional analyses on the data collected in an earlier Federal Motor Carrier Safety Administration (FMCSA) study of the effects of fatigue on drivers in local/short-haul operations.

In connection to this report, researchers were tasked by the FMCSA to investigate fatigue as a naturally occurring phenomenon by identifying and characterizing episodes of drowsiness that occurred during every period of driving. In addition, the researchers were to determine the operational or driving-environment factors associated with drowsy driving.

A total of 2,745 drowsy events were identified in approximately 900 total hours of naturalistic driving video data. Higher levels of fatigue were found to be associated with younger and less experienced drivers. In addition, a strong and consistent relationship was found between drowsiness and the time of day. Drowsy driving events were twice as likely to occur between 6 a.m. and 9 a.m., as compared to baseline, or non-fatigued driving, and approximately 30 percent of all observed instances of drowsiness occurred in the first hour of the work shift.

This report will be interesting both for motor carrier managers and for drivers as they deal with everyday fatigue issues in the commercial motor vehicle business.

NOTICE

SI* (MODERN METRIC) CONVERSION FACTORS

Table of APPROXIMATE CONVERSIONS TO SI UNITS

Symbol	When You Know	Multiply By	To Find	Symbol
		LENGTH		
in	inches	25.4	Millimeters	mm
ft	feet	0.305	Meters	m
yd	yards	0.914	Meters	m
mi	miles	1.61	Kilometers	km
		AREA		
in²	square inches	645.2	square millimeters	mm²
ft²	square feet	0.093	square meters	m²
yd²	square yards	0.836	square meters	m²
ac	acres	0.405	Hectares	ha
mi²	square miles	2.59	square kilometers	km²
		VOLUME	1000 L shall be shown in m³	
fl oz	fluid ounces	29.57	Milliliters	mL
gal	gallons	3.785	Liters	L
ft³	cubic feet	0.028	cubic meters	m³
yd³	cubic yards	0.765	cubic meters	m³
		MASS		
oz	ounces	28.35	Grams	g
b	pounds	0.454	Kilograms	kg
T	short tons (2000 lb)	0.907	megagrams (or "metric ton")	Mg (or "t")
		TEMPERATURE	Temperature is in exact degrees	
°F	Fahrenheit	$5 \times (F-32) \div 9$ or $(F-32) \div 1.8$	Celsius	°C
		ILLUMINATION		
fc	foot-candles	10.76	Lux	lx
fl	foot-Lamberts	3.426	candela/m²	cd/m²
		Force and Pressure or Stress		
bf	poundforce	4.45	Newtons	N
bf/in²	poundforce per square inch	6.89	Kilopascals	kPa

Table of APPROXIMATE CONVERSIONS FROM SI UNITS

Symbol	When You Know	Multiply By	To Find	Symbol
		LENGTH		
Mm	millimeters	0.039	inches	in
M	meters	3.28	feet	ft
m	meters	1.09	yards	yd
km	kilometers	0.621	miles	mi
		AREA		
mm²	square millimeters	0.0016	square inches	in²
m²	square meters	10.764	square feet	ft²
m²	square meters	1.195	square yards	yd²
ha	hectares	2.47	acres	ac
km²	square kilometers	0.386	square miles	mi²
		VOLUME		
mL	milliliters	0.034	fluid ounces	fl oz
L	liters	0.264	gallons	gal
m³	cubic meters	35.314	cubic feet	ft³
m³	cubic meters	1.307	cubic yards	yd³
		MASS		
g	grams	0.035	ounces	oz
kg	kilograms	2.202	pounds	b
Mg (or "t")	megagrams (or "metric ton")	1.103	short tons (2000 lb)	T
		TEMPERATURE	Temperature is in exact degrees	
°C	Celsius	$1.8c + 32$	Fahrenheit	°F
		ILLUMINATION		
lx	lux	0.0929	foot-candles	fc
cd/m²	candela/m²	0.2919	foot-Lamberts	fl
		Force & Pressure Or Stress		
N	newtons	0.225	poundforce	bf
kPa	kilopascals	0.145	poundforce per square inch	bf/in²

* SI is the symbol for the International System of Units. Appropriate rounding should be made to comply with Section 4 of ASTM E380.
(Revised March 2003, Section 508-accessible version September 2009)

TABLE OF CONTENTS

LIST OF TABLES

LIST OF FIGURES

ABBREVIATIONS, ACRONYMS, AND SYMBOLS

ANOVA	analysis of variance
CMV	commercial motor vehicle
DFAS	Driver Fatigue and Alertness Study
EYETRANS	The number of eye transitions (i.e., glances from one direction to another) made by the driver over the interval, indicating inattention
EYESOFF	The proportion of time during the interval that the driver was looking away from the forward roadway, indicating inattention
FMCSA	Federal Motor Carrier Safety Administration
L/SH	long/short haul
LOS	load of service, level or volume of traffic
mi/h	miles per hour
ORD	observed rating of drowsiness
PERCLOS	The proportion of time that the driver's eyes are closed or nearly closed during the measurement interval, indicating fatigue or drowsiness

EXECUTIVE SUMMARY

The Federal Motor Carrier Safety Administration (FMCSA) is focused on reducing crashes, injuries, and fatalities involving large trucks and buses. One element in meeting FMCSA's strategic safety objectives is an emphasis on the safety performance of commercial drivers to ensure that they are physically qualified to operate commercial motor vehicles safely while staying mentally alert. The purpose of this study is to characterize episodes of driver drowsiness and to assess the impact of drowsiness on driving performance using the naturalistic data of local/short-haul (L/SH) truck drivers. The results of the study will help to provide a better understanding of the relationship between fatigue or drowsiness and the safety of driver behavior and performance (for the purposes of this project, the terms "drowsiness" and "fatigue" are used synonymously). It is hoped that this information will be useful in identifying effective countermeasures for drowsy driving that will reduce the number of commercial vehicle-related fatalities and injuries. The primary objectives of the study were to:

- Investigate fatigue as a naturally occurring phenomenon by characterizing episodes of drowsiness that occurred during every period of driving for the L/SH data set.

- Characterize the natural occurrence of fatigue and drowsiness, and determine whether episodes of drowsiness are associated with operational or driving environment factors.

- Explore the effects of fatigue and drowsiness on safe driving performance.

- Identify relationships between fatigue, distraction, and safe driver behavior and performance.

The data used in this study were collected as part of a naturalistic field study of driver drowsiness among L/SH truck operators. L/SH operations can be defined as those primarily involving trips of 100 miles or less from the home base. Thus, L/SH drivers typically start and end their workdays at their home base. A total of 42 drivers from two L/SH trucking companies participated in the field study, in which in-service L/SH trucks were instrumented with data collection equipment. Each driver drove an instrumented truck for approximately 2 weeks. The instrumentation consisted of sensors to monitor vehicle parameters (i.e., velocity, lateral and longitudinal acceleration, steering position, and brake pedal activation. Each truck was also equipped with video cameras that provided exterior views of the driving environment and interior images of the driver's face. The cameras were activated upon engine ignition; video data were recorded continuously while the trucks were in operation, rather than being recorded only when triggered by pre-defined critical events or near-crash situations. Thus, the L/SH data set is a very rich source of naturalistic data for analyzing driving behavior and human factors issues.

The comprehensive study of commercial driver drowsiness consisted of four major tasks:

- Process the L/SH continuous video data to identify all episodes of fatigue/drowsiness.

- Characterize drowsiness and its relationship to driver and external factors.

- Relate driver drowsiness to driver performance.

- Relate driver drowsiness to driver distraction.

All instances of driver drowsiness were identified, and relationships between driver drowsiness and operational/external factors, driver performance, and driver distraction were investigated. Predictive models were developed to determine the driver characteristics (e.g., age, years of commercial driving experience, sleep quality/quantity) and external or environmental factors (e.g., time of day, weather, traffic density) that influence the likelihood of driver fatigue and drowsiness occurring on the job. Several analytical techniques, including analysis of variance, contingency table analysis, multiple linear regression, and logistic regression, were applied, and these methodologies produced generally consistent results.

A total of 2,745 drowsy events were identified in approximately 900 total hours of driving. Thus, the rate of drowsy occurrences for all drivers combined was 3.1 events per hour of driving. On a per-driver basis, the drowsiness rate varied from 0 to 9.3 events per hour. For each drowsiness event, analysts recorded the duration and assigned an Observer Rating of Drowsiness (ORD) based on a scale of 2 (slightly drowsy) to 5 (extremely drowsy). An ORD value of 1 is, by definition, considered to be a baseline, or non-drowsy, event. The breakdown of drowsy events by severity was as follows: 1,636 ORD 2 events (slightly drowsy); 824 ORD 3 events (moderately drowsy); 160 ORD 4 events (very drowsy); and 125 ORD 5 events (extremely drowsy).

A simple frequency count of drowsy events does not include the severity of drowsiness (e.g., a short yawn vs. multiple complete eye closures) nor does it take into account the amount of driving done by each driver. Therefore, a measure of drowsiness called the Fatigue Index was developed for each driver in this study. The Fatigue Index accounts for the frequency of occurrence of drowsy episodes, normalized by total driving time, as well as the severity of the drowsiness event. It is defined as the sum of the ORD rating for each drowsiness event, divided by the total number of hours of driving data analyzed. The Fatigue Index was used to classify drivers in two categories, a "High Fatigue" group and a "Low Fatigue" group. High fatigue, or drowsiness, was found to be associated with younger and less experienced drivers. Odds ratios estimated using logistic regression indicated that drivers in the 19–25-year-old age group were nine times more likely to be classified in the High Fatigue group than older drivers. Similarly, inexperienced drivers, with less than 1 year of commercial driving experience, were about seven times more likely to be High Fatigue drivers than those with more driving experience.

One of the major findings of this study was that every analysis provided evidence of a strong association between drowsiness and time of day. The early-morning time period between 6 a.m. and 9 a.m. was especially problematic for the L/SH drivers. Logistic regression results showed that drowsiness was twice as likely to occur between 6 a.m. and 9 a.m., and a linear regression model indicated a significant relationship between this time period and an increase in the proportion of time over the 3-minute event interval that the driver's eyes were closed or nearly closed (PERCLOS), the primary measure of drowsiness used in this study. Conversely, a decrease in PERCLOS (i.e., increased alertness) was associated with the time period between 12 p.m. and 3 p.m. These results, together with the finding that approximately 30 percent of all observed instances of drowsiness occurred within the first hour of the work shift, suggest that drivers may not be fully refreshed and awake when they begin their workday.

In addition, a somewhat weak association between sleep quantity, quality, and drowsy driving was established in this study. Analysis of variance results showed a significantly lower average sleep duration, as measured by Actiwatch data, on the nights preceding drowsy events, compared to baseline events. And drivers' self-reported subjective assessments of sleep quality were positively related to increases in PERCLOS in linear regression models. The absence of a stronger link between sleep behavior and driver drowsiness can most likely be attributed to the nature of the sleep data obtained during the L/SH field test. Due to the unreliability of the Actiwatch wrist monitor, usable information about actual sleep duration was lost for several of the L/SH drivers. Also, time spent in bed, a surrogate measure of sleep quantity, turned out to be a poor predictor of driver drowsiness.

This study provided a better understanding of the relationship between driver fatigue or drowsiness and driver distraction and inattention. Quantitative evidence was obtained to verify the hypothesis that drivers suffering from fatigue and/or drowsiness experience "tunnel vision." When a driver becomes drowsy, the rate of eye transitions and the proportion of time his/her eyes are off the forward roadway were both found to decrease. Therefore, a drowsy driver is less aware of the driving environment around him/her, and his/her ability to recognize potential hazards from other vehicles or objects outside the vehicle is compromised. This study also found that driving conditions such as poor visibility and undivided highways tend to increase the driver's focus on the forward roadway. Observation of driver behavior from the continuous video data revealed that in the majority of cases, drowsiness occurred during periods of extremely low driver workload brought on by boredom and monotony. In these cases, the driver would often respond by engaging in either secondary activities typically associated with driver distraction or drowsiness countermeasure activities in an effort to become more alert. Drowsiness countermeasures such as rubbing the face and neck, stretching and shifting in the seat, and singing along with the radio, were observed much more frequently during periods of drowsiness than during alert driving. On the other hand, secondary activities that demand a great deal of driver attention, such as eating, reading, and using a wireless phone, occurred predominantly when the driver was awake and alert. Drivers must continually allocate attention to competing tasks, both driving and non-driving. This study provided some interesting insights into how drivers handle competing tasks and how they respond to situations when they feel drowsy or fatigued. Still, few quantitative data exist to characterize the relationship between driver workload, distraction, and drowsiness. Providing a better understanding of this relationship could be an area for further research.

And finally, two measures of driver performance—lane-keeping and speed management—were evaluated in an effort to correlate driver drowsiness and performance. Because lane tracking sensors were not included in the onboard instrumentation system in the L/SH field study, investigation of a driver's lane-keeping performance was limited to observational analysis of video data. Gross violations and obvious lane excursions were apparent in the video data, but variations in vehicle position within the lane and minor lane drifting were not easily detectable. In this study, an event having an ORD value of 5 is defined as one that has an impact on driving ability or performance. The overwhelming majority of ORD 5 events involved lane violations; thus, the frequency and rate of occurrence of ORD 5 events can give a rough idea of the extent to which drowsiness affects a driver's ability to maintain lane position. A total of 125 ORD 5 events were observed, or 4.5 percent of the total number of drowsy events identified in this study. Of the 41 drivers who participated in the L/SH study, 19 showed signs of impaired driving performance due to drowsiness, and for all drivers collectively, the rate of occurrence of ORD 5 events is about one event for every 7 hours of driving. The results of an analysis of speed variations during periods of drowsy driving were inconclusive. No compelling evidence was found in this study to suggest that a driver's ability to maintain and control vehicle speed is severely impacted by drowsiness.

This study provided an analytical framework for quantitatively assessing driver drowsiness as a function of driver characteristics and the driving environment. It is recommended that this work be the basis for a follow-on study to develop a more robust and comprehensive predictor of drowsiness using a combination of physiological data (e.g., PERCLOS) with other driver and vehicle performance data (e.g., lane-keeping, speed variation, time-to-collision). Current drowsy-driver warning systems incorporate PERCLOS as the primary measure of drowsiness. However, the PERCLOS monitor has some operational limitations and deficiencies; for example, it does not work reliably in daylight, or for drivers who wear eyeglasses. Therefore, it becomes important to consider what other indicators could be used to warn a driver that he/she is becoming drowsy when the PERCLOS fatigue monitor is not available or is not performing reliably. A future investigation is recommended to set up equations to predict PERCLOS on the basis of performance measures such as lane position, speed variation, and position relative to forward vehicles, and to develop an algorithm that incorporates physiological data as well as vehicle/driver performance data into a drowsy-driver warning system.

1. INTRODUCTION

The Federal Motor Carrier Safety Administration (FMCSA) is focused on reducing crashes, injuries, and fatalities involving large trucks and buses. FMCSA has established a safety goal of reducing the number of deaths and injuries resulting from commercial-vehicle-related crashes. One element in meeting FMCSA's strategic safety objectives is an emphasis on the safety performance of commercial drivers, to ensure that they are physically qualified to operate commercial motor vehicles safely while staying mentally alert. The objective of this study is to characterize episodes of driver drowsiness and to assess the impact of driver drowsiness on driving performance using the naturalistic data of local/short-haul (L/SH) truck drivers. The results of the study will help to provide a better understanding of the relationship between drowsiness, and the safety of driver behavior and performance (for the purposes of this project, the terms "drowsiness" and "fatigue" are used synonymously). It is hoped that this information will be useful in identifying effective countermeasures for drowsy driving that will reduce the number of commercial vehicle-related fatalities and injuries, in keeping with FMCSA's strategic safety goal.

Driver drowsiness is a safety issue of special concern to commercial motor vehicle (CMV) transportation. FMCSA, the CMV industry, highway safety advocates and researchers, and the general public have all identified driver drowsiness as a high-priority commercial vehicle safety issue. Because of their greater mileage exposure and other factors, commercial drivers' risk of being involved in a drowsiness -related crash is far greater than that of non-commercial drivers, even though CMV drivers represent a relatively small proportion of all drivers involved in drowsiness -related crashes and their rate of involvement per mile traveled is no greater than that of non-commercial drivers (Wylie, Shultz, Miller, Mitler, & Mackie, 1996b). Moreover, other contributing crash factors such as alcohol, speeding, and other unsafe driving practices are less common among commercial drivers and thus less important relative to drowsiness. Previous research (Wylie, Shultz, Miller, Mitler, and Mackie 1996a) has indicated that the primary causes of driver drowsiness among long-haul commercial vehicle operators include time-of-day, time-on-task, and sleep debt. In addition, driver drowsiness is also associated with driving in darkness, adverse weather, monotonous driving environments, physical work, and noise/heat/vibration inside the cab. A list of other potential drowsiness -related factors has been cited by L/SH drivers, such as lack of sleep, hard/physical workday, time spent waiting to unload, irregular meal times, and long hours of work (Hanowski, Wierwille, Gellatly, Early, and Dingus 1998).

As part of its study on the impact of L/SH trucking operations on driver drowsiness, data was collected from an on-road field study in which in-service L/SH trucks were instrumented with data collection equipment (Hanowski, Wierwille, Garness, & Dingus, 2000). The onboard instrumentation consisted of sensors to monitor such vehicle performance parameters as velocity, lateral and longitudinal acceleration, steering position, and brake pedal activation. Each truck was also equipped with video cameras that provided exterior views of the driving environment and interior images of the driver's face. A total of 42 drivers from 2 L/SH trucking companies participated in the field study, and each driver drove an instrumented truck for approximately 2 weeks. The video cameras were activated upon engine ignition and video data were recorded continuously while the trucks were in operation, rather than being recorded only when triggered by pre-defined critical events or near-crash situations. Thus, the L/SH data set is a very rich source of naturalistic data for analyzing driving behavior and human-factors issues.

The researchers conducted a comprehensive study of commercial driver drowsiness by analyzing the continuous video data acquired during the L/SH naturalistic driving field test. The primary objectives of the study were to:

- Investigate drowsiness as a naturally occurring phenomenon by characterizing episodes of drowsiness that occurred during every periods of driving for the L/SH data set

- Characterize the natural occurrence of drowsiness, and determine whether episodes of drowsiness are associated with operational or driving-environment factors

- Explore the effects of drowsiness on safe driving performance

- Identify relationships between drowsiness, distraction, and safe driver behavior and performance

The research effort documented in this report expanded on an earlier study of L/SH driver drowsiness in several important ways. The previous study, (Hanowski et al., 2000), focused only on critical incidents. In the current study, instances of driver drowsiness were identified that occurred during all periods of driving, not just those occurrences that resulted in a critical or near-crash event. Furthermore, once these drowsiness events were identified, the relationship of driver drowsiness to the following factors was investigated:

- Operational and external factors.

- Driver performance.

- Driver distraction.

Each of these three areas can be investigated separately; however, when combined, they also form a logical progression of analysis from a general characterization of drowsiness to more detailed analyses of drowsiness -related factors.

1.1 PREVIOUS RESEARCH ON COMMERCIAL DRIVER DROWSINESS

Since driver drowsiness is a critical CMV safety issue, a number of research studies have previously been conducted to address the area of driver alertness and fatigue or drowsiness. The Driver Fatigue and Alertness Study (DFAS), a comprehensive over-the-road field study of commercial driver alertness, was a collaborative effort involving the Federal Highway Administration's Office of Motor Carriers (now FMCSA), Transport Canada, the Trucking Research Institute of the American Trucking Associations, three motor carriers, and other research and industry associations (Wylie, Shultz, Miller, Mitler, & Mackie , 1996b). The study consisted of 4 different driving schedules, 80 drivers, and more than 200,000 miles of highway driving. Numerous measures of the drivers' alertness and performance were taken during driving periods, and their physiological condition was also monitored during off-duty sleep periods. Major findings from the DFAS included:

- Driver alertness and performance were more consistently related to time-of-day than to time-on-task.

- Although it is not applicable to the L/SH driver population used in the current study, drowsiness episodes were found to be eight times more likely between midnight and 6 a.m. than at other times.

- Drivers' stated self-assessments of their levels of alertness did not correlate closely with objective measures of performance, indicating that drivers are not reliable judges of their levels of drowsiness.

- Significant individual differences in levels of alertness and performance were observed among drivers.

As an adjunct to the DFAS, to extend prior research and to collect additional data about CMV drivers and their job characteristics, a survey was designed and conducted to determine the prevalence of factors that may contribute to drowsiness in CMV drivers and to identify and assess the methods used by drivers to counter drowsiness or its symptoms (Abrams, Shultz, & Wylie, 1997). The survey questionnaire was given to 511 long-haul tractor-trailer drivers, and the results showed that drivers use a variety of methods and activities for maintaining alertness while driving. Some of the more common activities include:

- Cooling the truck cab by air conditioning or opening windows.

- Stretching or changing sitting positions.

- Listening to the radio or tapes.

- Talking on the CB radio.

- Drinking coffee.

- Eating.

- Smoking.

- Singing.

Many of these activities are considered to be driver distractions; however, they may serve a useful purpose by increasing a driver's workload and returning the driver to a state of alertness after a period of fatigue or drowsiness. This relationship between driver drowsiness and driver distraction is explored further in this study.

The Federal Highway Administration's Office of Motor Carriers, which is now FMCSA, sponsored a research project to characterize the operating practices of CMV drivers and to assess the relationship of these practices to driver fatigue (O'Neill, Krueger, Van Hemel, & McGowan, 1999). One aspect of this project was a driving simulator study designed to investigate: (1) driver performance under a sustained 14-hours-on-duty/10-hours-off-duty schedule over a 15-day period, and (2) the fatigue-related decline in driving performance resulting from loading and unloading cargo. Researchers found that a slight degradation of driver performance in crash-likely situations occurred in the mid-afternoon, but there were improvements after each break, whether for rest, meals, or loading/unloading activities. In addition, the assessment of physical loading/unloading activities on driver performance produced mixed results. Drivers performed two 90-minute loading/unloading sessions during the driving day, one in the morning and one in the afternoon. After the morning session, there was an improvement in driver response to simulated crash-likely situations, probably due to a short-term invigorating effect associated with physical exercise and a break in the driving routine. The afternoon loading/unloading session, on the other hand, did not have the same effect on drivers. Driving performance deteriorated more rapidly after the afternoon session, suggesting that physical and/or general fatigue/drowsiness and time-of-day effects are sufficient to overpower some short-term effects of a change in activity. Driving performance was seen to return to starting levels near the end of the day.

During an analytical study to characterize the L/SH driver fatigue crash problem, (Massie, Blower, & Campbell, 1998), researchers developed several definitions of L/SH vs. over-the-road trucks and examined the prevalence of driver fatigue as a principal factor in truck crashes. Data sources included the 1992 Truck Inventory and Use Survey and 1991–1993 Trucks Involved in Fatal Accidents crash files. L/SH trucks in these crash data files were defined based on vehicle size (i.e., Class 3–6 single-unit straight trucks) and/or by operational nature (i.e., trip length). Trip distance was found to have the most pronounced effect on the percentage of fatal crashes that were fatigue-related; shorter trips are associated with a much lower incidence of fatal crashes. The risk of L/SH truck involvement in fatigue-related fatal crashes is a fraction of the risk for over-the-road or long-haul trucks. A much larger naturalistic driving study of L/SH driver fatigue was conducted and will be discussed in the following section.

1.2   LOCAL/SHORT HAUL DRIVER FATIGUE STUDY

The data used in this study were collected as part of a naturalistic field study of driver drowsiness among local/short haul truck operators. Local/short haul (L/SH) operations can be defined as those that primarily involve trips of 100 miles or less from the home base. Thus, L/SH drivers typically start and end their workdays at their home base. To investigate the issues of drowsiness and general safety in L/SH trucking operations, a two-phased research effort was conducted (Hanowski et al., 2000). Phase I involved focus groups to gain an understanding of the general safety concerns related to L/SH trucking and, in particular, the degree to which drowsiness plays a role. Phase II consisted of a field study in which L/SH trucks were instrumented with data collection equipment and driven by L/SH drivers as they worked their normal delivery routes.

Data from the focus groups were analyzed, and a list of critical safety issues was generated and ranked in order of importance. Results indicated that driver fatigue or drowsiness was the fifth-highest-ranked safety issue, behind:

- Problems caused by drivers of light vehicles.
- Stress due to time pressure.
- Inattention.
- Roadway/dock design.

Drivers also discussed fatigue- and drowsiness-related issues, and prioritized and ranked the issues in terms of importance. The most important issues included inadequate sleep, hard

4

physical workday, heat and/or no air conditioning in truck cab, waiting to unload, irregular meal times and work shifts, and long hours of work.

Findings from the focus group effort also suggested that, although drivers report that drowsiness is an issue in L/SH trucking, they do not perceive it to be as critical as it is in long-haul trucking. L/SH drivers typically work during daylight hours and have work breaks that interrupt their driving. Compared to long-haul truck drivers, whose primary task is operating the vehicle and who therefore drive uninterrupted for long stretches, L/SH drivers perform a variety of tasks during the workday. Throughout the L/SH field study, at the end of each work shift, drivers completed a questionnaire that provided information about the specific activities they performed during their workday. It was determined that, as a group, the drivers spent approximately 28 percent of their day driving, 35 percent loading/unloading, 26 percent on other work-related assignments (e.g., merchandising, checking in/out, vehicle inspection, etc.), 7 percent waiting to unload, 2 percent eating, 0.5 percent resting, and 1.5 percent on other activities (Wylie et al., 1996b).

The focus group effort provided important data for understanding what drivers view as the critical safety and drowsiness -related issues in the L/SH trucking industry. Researchers complemented the subjective information obtained in the focus groups with objective data collected during an over-the-road field study. Two trucking companies and a total of 42 drivers participated in the field study. Each driver drove an instrumented vehicle for approximately 2 weeks. All the drivers were male; they ranged from 19 to 57 years old, with an average age of 31 years. The onboard instrumentation consisted of sensors to monitor such vehicle performance parameters as velocity, lateral and longitudinal acceleration, steering position, and brake pedal activation, as well as a video camera system that provided exterior views of the driving environment and interior images of the driver's face. Five video cameras were used in the L/SH field study:

- A forward-looking camera that captured the forward road scene, traffic situation, and possible incidents.

- A rear-looking camera to capture the traffic situation behind the vehicle and to assist in incident detection.

- Left-side.

- Right-side cameras mounted on the side mirrors and aimed toward the rear.

- A driver's face camera mounted inside the cab on either the driver's left or right to pick up facial expressions, eyelid closure, glance location, and head turns.

The five camera images were multiplexed into a single image on the videos, and a timestamp legend ("sync" number) was also included in the video frame. The sync number is critical for determining event start times and durations (one sync number = 0.1 second), and vehicle performance data measured by onboard instrumentation are matched to the video data using the sync number.

In its on-road field study of L/SH driver fatigue (Hanowski et al., 2000), researchers focused only on critical incidents. A critical incident was defined as "an event that, in the opinion of the analyst, either was nearly a crash such that the driver of one or more of the vehicles involved was required to take immediate evasive action to avoid a crash, or put the driver of the vehicle in a dangerous situation that may have resulted in a crash." Researchers identified a total of 249 critical incidents from the L/SH field study. Of these, 137 were attributed to other drivers, 77 were attributed to the L/SH drivers, 20 were categorized as incidents in which the L/SH driver was involved only as an observer, and 15 incidents occurred as a result of the L/SH driver responding to another type of situation, such as an animal in the road. Fatigue was determined to be a contributing factor in 16 incidents (20.8 percent) where the L/SH driver was judged to be at fault. Of the 77 critical incidents attributed to L/SH drivers, it is interesting to note that just 8 of the 42 drivers accounted for 60 percent of the incidents. Thus, the majority of driver-at-fault incidents involved a minority (19 percent) of the participating drivers. Furthermore, younger and less experienced drivers were significantly more likely to be involved in critical incidents than were older and more experienced drivers. Younger and less experienced drivers also exhibited higher on-the-job drowsiness.

Rather than focusing on crashes and near-crash events, the primary objective of the current research study on L/SH driver fatigue is to investigate drowsiness (for the purposes of this project, the terms "drowsiness" and "fatigue" are used synonymously) as a naturally occurring phenomenon by characterizing episodes of drowsiness that occurred during every period of driving in the L/SH data set.

2. RESEARCH METHODOLOGY

2.1 VIDEO DATA REDUCTION

The video data reduction effort for this project was a two-stage process. Task 1 consisted of reviewing the video data and identifying all drowsiness events. Task 2 involved detailed analysis of a subset of drowsiness events identified during Task 1. This section discusses the methods used to accomplish these two data reduction tasks.

The L/SH data set consists of 414 videotapes and approximately 908 hours of video footage. Forty-two drivers participated in the L/SH study. In Task 1, analysts reviewed the entire video library to document every observed occurrence of drowsiness. The following are samples of the more prominent driver behaviors that were characteristic of drowsiness events: yawning, rubbing eyes, closing eyes, slow blinks, bobbing head, and verbal announcement of drowsiness state. When a drowsiness event was identified, the analyst recorded the driver number, tape number, and video sync number corresponding to the beginning and end of the event. In reviewing the event, the analyst assessed the drowsiness level of the driver during the event, using a five-point scale titled Observer Rating of Drowsiness (ORD). On a per-driver basis, the drowsiness rate varied from 0 to 9.3 events per hour. For each fatigue event, analysts recorded the duration and assigned an ORD based on a scale of 2 (slightly drowsy) to 5 (extremely drowsy). An ORD value of 1 is, by definition, considered to be a baseline, or non-fatigued, event. The method used to determine this rating scale and the reliability, consistency, and validity of the drowsiness assessment procedure are discussed by Wierwille and Ellsworth (1994). Versions of this scale have been used in previous studies, including the L/SH fatigue study (Hanowski et al., 2000) and a study of the impact of sleeper berth usage on driver fatigue (Dingus et al., 2002). The scale provides a subjective rating of how drowsy the analyst believes the driver is during the event (see Table 1). The ORD rating was used to prioritize the drowsiness events by severity. The more detailed data reduction in Task 2 relied upon these ratings for event selection.

The task of reviewing the video data involved using computer workstations that had an attached video monitor and a VCR. Analysts manually reviewed every frame of the approximately 900 hours of videotape and documented all drowsiness events. After making this first pass through the tapes, analysts made a second pass focusing on events identified by other analysts. That is, each analyst was provided with a list of identified events (from the first pass), and their task was to conduct a validity check on these events. The purpose of this second pass was to help ensure reliability between analysts and to double-check the drowsiness events and the assigned ORD ratings (see Table 1).

Table 1. ORD Rating Scale

ORD Rating	Drowsiness
1	Not Drowsy. Driver shows no signs of being drowsy.
2	Slightly Drowsy. Driver shows minor signs of being drowsy (single yawn, single stretch, droopy eyelids for a short period of time), but quickly recovers. This does not have any impact on the driver's ability to drive.
3	Moderately Drowsy. Driver shows signs of being drowsy (yawns, stretches, moves around in seat, droopy eyelids for a slightly longer period of time, minor blinking), and takes slightly longer to recover. This does not have any impact on the driver's ability to drive.
4	Very Drowsy. Driver shows signs of being drowsy (yawns often, has very heavy/droopy eyelids, frequent blinking), and the duration lasts much longer. This does not have any impact on the driver's ability to drive.
5	Extremely Drowsy. Driver shows extreme signs of being drowsy (yawns often, has very heavy/droopy eyelids, has trouble keeping eyes open, very frequent blinking), and the duration lasts much longer. This has an impact on the driver's ability to drive.

An event was judged to have commenced when a characteristic drowsiness behavior was observed (for example, a yawn). The video sync number of the initial drowsiness behavior was noted as the event's start time. In some cases, the event would end shortly thereafter; for example, the driver would scan the environment before making a lane change maneuver. At other times, the driver's level of drowsiness would build until an alerting event occurred to reduce the driver's level of drowsiness. This is illustrated schematically in Figure 1. This chart shows that the level of drowsiness starts out low and increases parabolically as time increases until the alerting event occurs at time $T = 0$. The drowsiness level decreases stepwise at this point back to the low level at which it started, and stays low for the remainder of the graph. The alerting event that returned the driver to a state of alert and attentive driving could be any number of things, including: making a lane change, making a right or left turn, becoming distracted by a passing vehicle, arriving at the delivery location, etc. The sync number associated with the alerting event was noted as the event's end time.

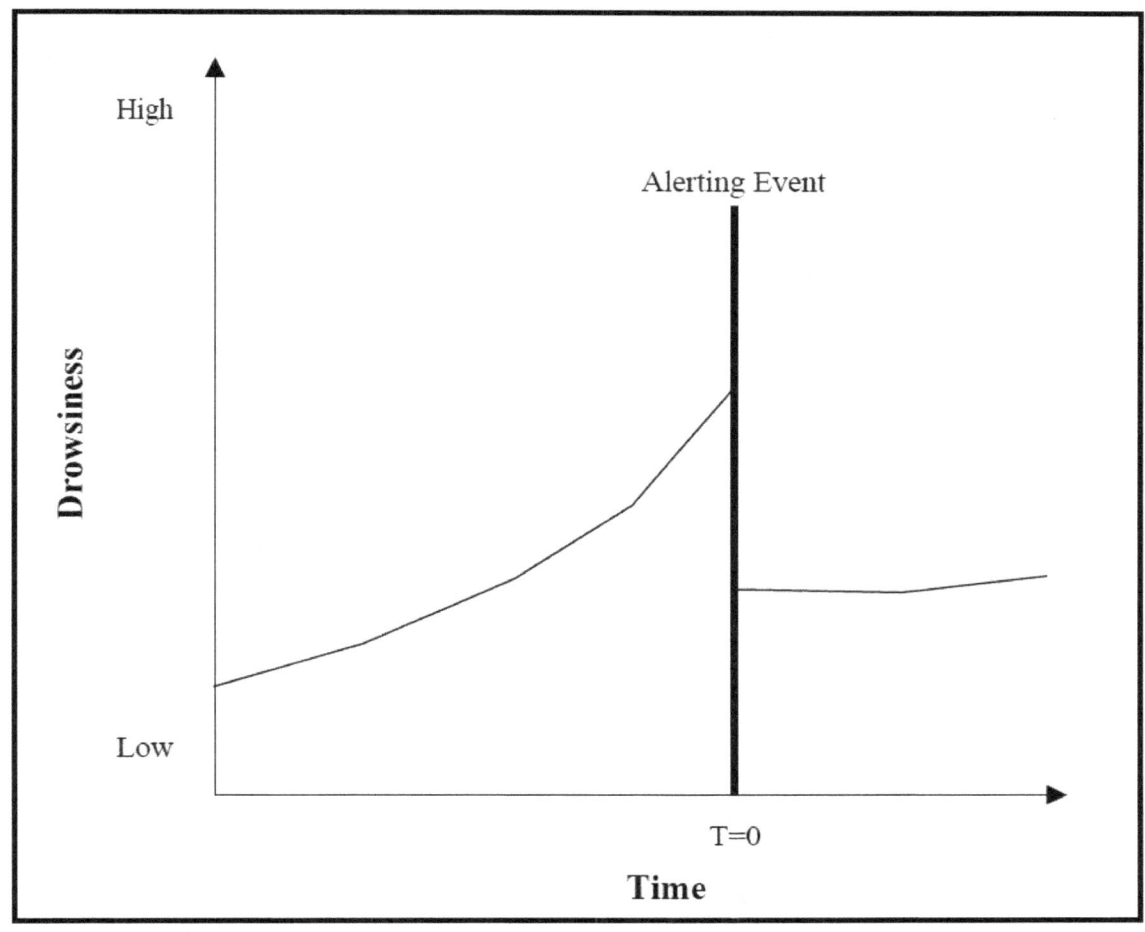

Figure 1. Drowsiness Events Ended with the Occurrence of an Alerting Event

It was previously stated that 908 hours of video data were reviewed. However, it should be noted that only 871 of these 908 hours were suitable for analysis. Thirty-seven hours of video were not analyzed because the video was too dark to see the driver, or the driver behind the wheel of the truck was not a consenting participant in the study. For example, occasional problems with the onboard cameras would result in a blank or very dark video recording. Additionally, on occasion, "relief" drivers would operate one of the study trucks, without having consented to participate in the study. In both of these situations, the data were not usable and could not be analyzed.

Task 2 involved detailed data reduction and analysis of drowsy-driving episodes that were identified in Task 1. Additionally, periods of "baseline" driving (e.g., those with an ORD value of 1, or non-drowsy driving behavior), in which the driver appeared alert and attentive to the driving task and did not exhibit any outward signs of fatigue, were also determined and analyzed. A total of 1,000 fatigue and baseline events were analyzed. After discussions between the researchers, it was decided that all of the high-severity events (i.e., those with ORD values of 4 or 5) would be analyzed, along with matching baseline events. The Task 1 video review identified 160 events with an ORD of 4 and 125 events with an ORD of 5. For each of these severe drowsiness events, a baseline event was selected and analyzed. The only explicit requirement for selecting baseline events was that they must be matched to drowsiness events by driver. While matching baseline events were randomly sampled, in some cases the dependent factor of interest dictated the baseline event selection process. For example, if an ORD 5 drowsiness event resulting in repeated lane violations is observed to occur on a curved roadway, then a baseline event on a curved road would also be chosen. This allows the analysis to determine whether fatigue and drowsiness, rather than the challenging road geometry, is the primary factor contributing to impaired driving performance. While every external factor cannot be controlled in a naturalistic driving study, keeping extraneous variables consistent between the drowsiness and baseline episodes as much as possible enabled the analysis to focus on the direct impact of drowsiness on driving performance. The remaining ORD 2 and 3 events were more or less randomly selected to reach the 1,000-event limit; however, the following ground rules or criteria were used in the selection process:

- Drivers who wore eyeglasses were excluded, since the reflected glare from the eyeglasses made PERCLOS and eye glance analyses very difficult.

- A 75:25 ratio of drowsiness -to-baseline events was arbitrarily selected so that more fatigue events would be sampled.

- An equal number of ORD 2 and ORD 3 events were selected for analysis. Task 1 analysis identified a total of 1,636 ORD 2 events and 824 ORD 3 events. Therefore, while ORD 3 events are slightly more severe and potentially more interesting drowsy episodes, they occur far less frequently than ORD 2 events. In the end, it was decided to select equal numbers of ORD 2 and 3 events.

- The events were proportionally allocated across the subject population so that drivers who exhibited signs of drowsiness more frequently received greater representation in the analysis sample than drivers who had fewer drowsy episodes.

- Events in which the driver was stopped in traffic or at a delivery destination during the 3 minutes prior to the end of the event were excluded; thus, the detailed event analysis (PERCLOS, the proportion of time that the driver's eyes are closed or nearly closed during the measurement interval; EYETRANS, the number of eye transitions (i.e., glances from one direction to another) made by the driver over the interval; and EYESOFF, the proportion of time during the interval that the driver was looking away from the forward roadway) was done only for periods of driving.

Table 2 shows the final breakdown of the 1,000 drowsiness events and their matching baseline events that were analyzed in Task 2.

**Table 2. Breakdown of Events
by ORD for Task 2 Analysis**

ORD Rating	Number of Fatigue Events	Number of Matched Baseline (ORD 1) Events
2	161	54
3	161	54
4	160	160
5	125	125
Total	**607**	**393**

The software program that was used in the event reduction and the steps followed in the analysis process are outlined below. Note that the software program used in the current effort was developed for the original L/SH project (Hanowski et al., 2000). The steps in the analysis process varied slightly between the two studies.

2.1.1 STEP 1: SETTNG UP THE EVENT

Setting up the event refers to locating a drowsiness event on the videotape and preparing it for reduction/archiving. Before setting up the event, the analyst began by logging into the software program and selecting the location of the data files to be analyzed (i.e., the directory in which the data files were stored). Once the correct data file was selected, the New Subject form, shown in Figure 2, was opened. This figure depicts the computer screen seen by the video analyst that is used to enter basic information prior to analyzing an event. Boxes for entering the subject number, the subject's age and gender, the shift number, the start sync number of the video event, and the date and time corresponding to the start of the event, are shown on the form. When the analyst finishes entering this information, he or she clicks the button labeled "Done" to proceed.

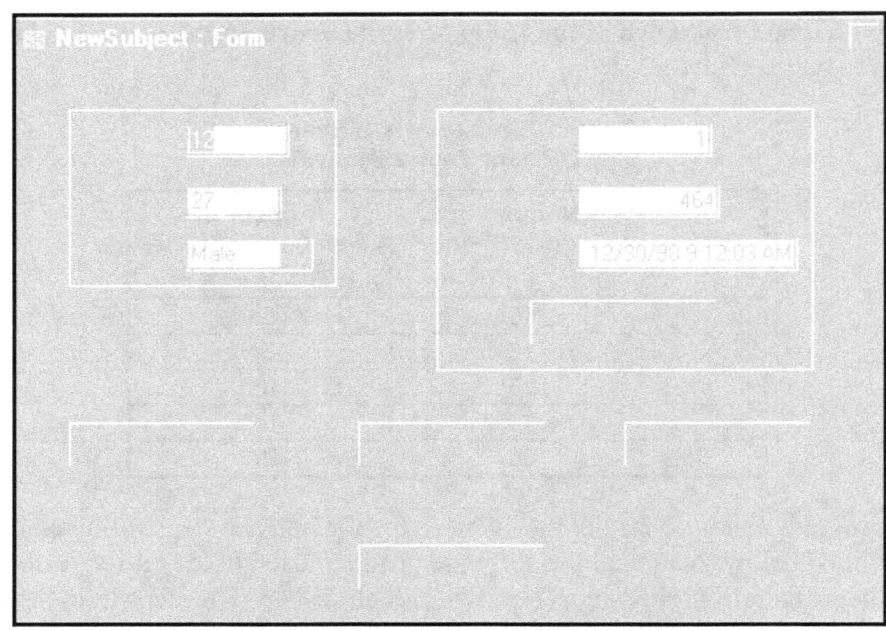

Figure 2. New Subject Form Used in Task 2 Event Data Reduction

In the original L/SH study, three different event types were of interest: critical incidents, backing episodes, and lane-change maneuvers. For the current study, drowsiness episodes were of interest. Because the outputs resulting from a critical-incident analysis and a drowsiness-episode analysis were similar, analysts in the current effort clicked the button labeled "Critical Incident" to analyze a drowsiness episode.

When a drowsiness episode was identified for analysis, the analyst filled in the fields of the Event Form, shown in Figure 3. This figure shows a computer screenshot of the form used by the video analyst to enter all relevant information describing the event being analyzed. At the top, the analyst enters the subject number, the subject's age and gender, and the type of truck driven. On the left side of the form are boxes for entering the following event information: Beginning sync value, 10 seconds before sync value, ending sync value, Observe sync value, duration, drowsiness level (i.e., ORD rating), Percent Closed (i.e., PERCLOS value), EYETRANS, and EYESOFF. In addition, the form has pull-down menus that the analyst uses to record the following parameters and road conditions observed on the video tape: Number of lanes (in one direction), driver's lane position, road type, road geometry, road surface condition, traffic density, weather, visibility, and illumination. Again, there is a "Done" button at the bottom of the form that the analyst clicks when the form is completed.

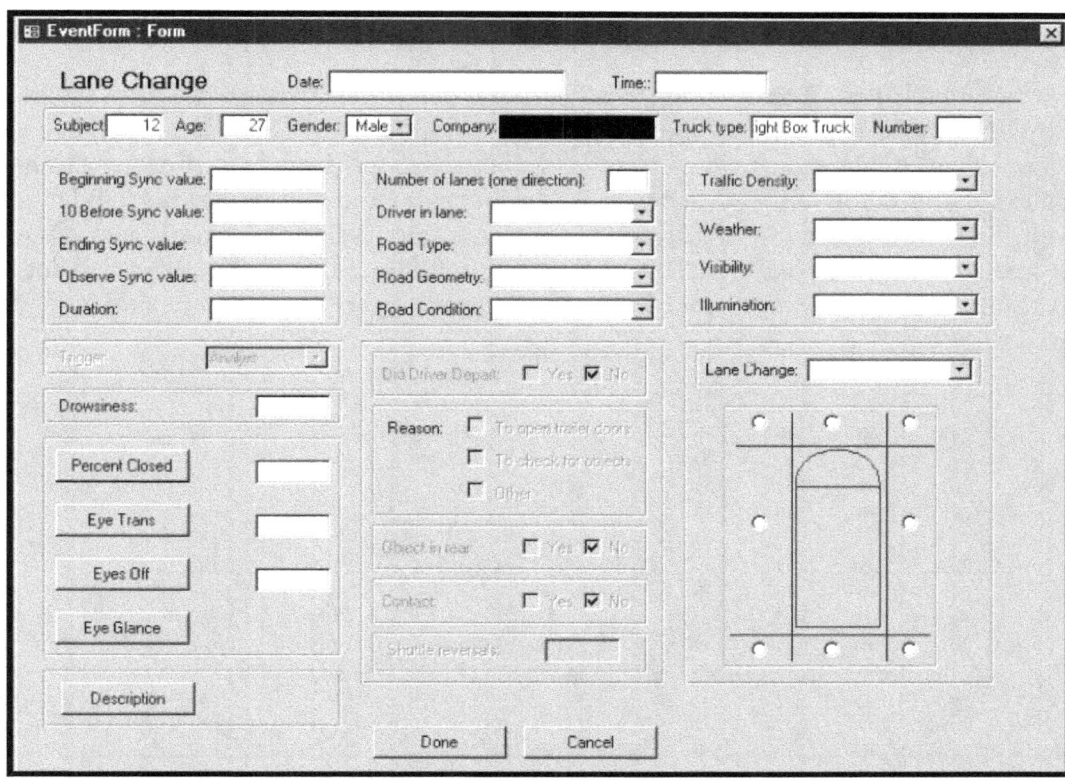

Figure 3. Event Form Used to Enter Data in the Reduction/Archiving Process

In the original L/SH study, the fields in this form changed slightly depending on the type of event being analyzed. For example, the field and diagram in the lower right corner labeled "Lane Change" was completed only for lane-change events. If a critical incident or backing event were being examined, this field was "grayed" and would not allow analyst input. As noted earlier, only drowsiness events (considered critical incidents by the software program) were analyzed; therefore, in the current study, the backing-event and lane-change-event fields were always grayed.

As can be seen in Figure 3, the analyst entered several information items, including the event date and time, subject number, age and gender of driver, the truck number and type, the sync number corresponding to the beginning of the event, the end-of-event sync number, the sync number corresponding to three minutes prior to the end of the event (used for drowsiness analyses), number of lanes, lane of travel, road type, road geometry, road condition, traffic density, weather, visibility, and illumination. When analyzing critical incidents in the original L/SH study, the analyst also specified the event trigger (i.e., vehicle sensor data trigger, critical incident button, or analyst's observation). For the current effort, the trigger was always the analyst's observation, since an analyst watching the video for observable signs of drowsiness determined each event.

2.2   STEP 2: DROWSINESS ASSESSMENT

The next step in the Task 2 data reduction/archiving process was to assess the drowsiness level of the driver from the beginning of the event to the end of the event. This duration ranged from a few seconds to 10 minutes or more, depending on how long the driver was drowsy. The analyst used the ORD scale shown in Figure 4 to make his/her assessment. It should be noted that an ORD value of 1 was automatically assigned to each baseline event. This chart simply shows a number line with the five possible ORD levels. From left to right, the levels are 1 for Not Drowsy, 2 for Slightly Drowsy, 3 for Moderately Drowsy, 4 for Very Drowsy, and 5 for Extremely Drowsy.

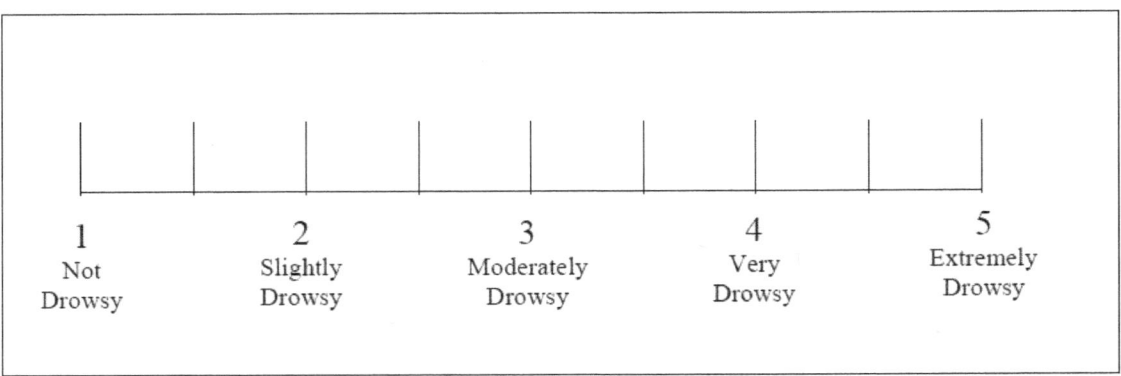

Figure 4. Drowsiness Scale Used by the Analysts

In addition to ORD, three other fatigue/inattention measures were determined for each drowsiness episode: PERCLOS (fatigue), EYETRANS (inattention), and EYESOFF (inattention). PERCLOS is defined as the proportion of time that the driver's eyes are closed or nearly closed during the measurement interval. EYETRANS is defined as the number of eye transitions (i.e., glances from one direction to another) made by the driver over the interval. And EYESOFF is the proportion of time during the interval that the driver was looking away from the forward roadway. Each of the three measures was calculated over a 3-minute interval. Using the alerting event as the drowsiness episode end point (see Figure 1), the analyst rewound the videotape for 3 minutes. From this point until the alerting event (T = 0), the analyst carefully reviewed the video and determined the values for PERCLOS, EYETRANS, and EYESOFF. Measures of EYETRANS and EYESOFF were also determined for each 3-minute baseline event.

Although previous research has described the validity of PERCLOS (Wierwille, 1999) and ORD—sometimes referred to as OBSERV—(Wierwille & Ellsworth, 1994), EYETRANS and EYESOFF were new measures that were used for the first time in the original L/SH study. The assumed validity of these measures is based on the hypothesis that multiple short glances (i.e., scanning) with a high proportion of glances to the forward view (i.e., road) are likely to result in attentive and safe driving. Although these measures have not been validated, it seems reasonable to suggest that drivers who take in frequent small samples of the environment, and devote the largest proportion of their time to the forward view, would appear to demonstrate a high level of attention to the driving task. It is also suggested that this higher level of attention would equate to safe driving.

The program form shown in Figure 5 was used to determine PERCLOS, or the proportion of time during the interval that the driver's eyes were closed or nearly closed. The "Program Form for Calculating PERCLOS" shows the computer screen the analyst uses while doing the PERCLOS analysis. The Observ Sync number, event duration in seconds, duration eyes closed in seconds, percent closed, and excluded time are all computed on this form. There is also a message for the analyst to press "c" on the computer keyboard while the driver's eyes are closed and press "x" to exclude time, along with a Start box to begin the analysis.

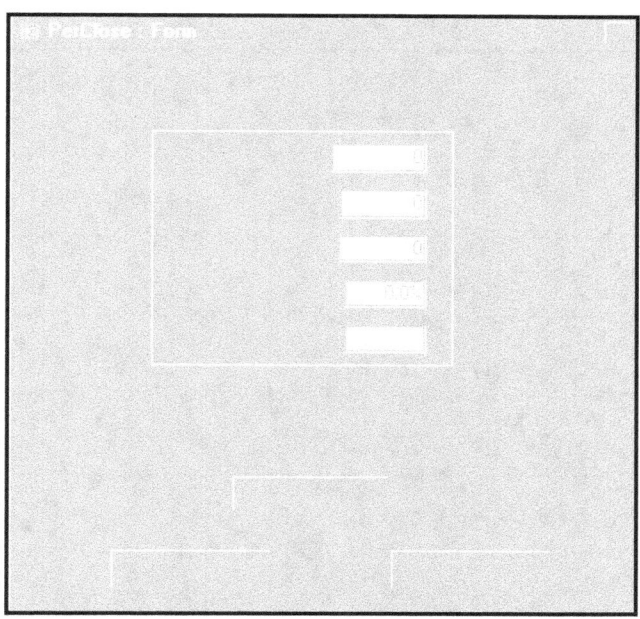

Figure 5. Program Form for Calculating PERCLOS

As can be seen in the PERCLOS form, the analyst typed in the "Observe Sync" value, or the sync number corresponding to the point in the video that was three minutes prior to the end of the drowsiness event (T=0). Based on the sync number for the alerting event (entered previously), the program automatically calculated the duration of the interval (i.e., approximately three minutes). Then, the analyst simultaneously started the video and clicked the Start button on the PERCLOS form. Whenever the driver's eyes were closed (80–100 percent closed), the analyst pressed the "c" key on the keyboard. Whenever the driver's eyes were open, the analyst released the "c" key. Whenever the analyst could not determine whether the driver's eyes were open or closed, he/she pressed the "x" key, which served to reduce the 3-minute interval for whatever length of time the "x" key was held down. At the end of the interval (i.e., when the sync number for the end of the event was reached), the program automatically shut off and calculated PERCLOS by determining the total length of time the "c" key was held down and dividing this value by total interval period. As shown in Figure 5, the program showed the analyst the total time that the driver's eyes were closed, the derived percent closed, and the excluded time (i.e., time that the "x" key was pressed down). When the analyst was satisfied that PERCLOS was determined correctly, he/she clicked the "Done" button on the program form and the PERCLOS analysis was saved. It should be noted that the program used the "proportion" definition of PERCLOS internally, but multiplied the value by 100 to display it as a percentage, as shown in Figure 5.

EYETRANS, the number of eye transitions made by the driver over the 3-minute interval, was the third drowsiness/inattention measure determined by analyzing the video tape. The process for the analyst in determining EYETRANS was similar to that for determining PERCLOS. Figure 6 shows the EYETRANS form that was used. This figure shows a computer screenshot of the form used to do EYETRANS analysis. The Observ Sync number, event duration in seconds, number of eye transitions, eye transition rate, and excluded time are all computed on this form. There is also a message for the analyst to press "t" on the computer keyboard when the driver's eyes transition and press "x" to exclude time, along with a Start box to begin the analysis.

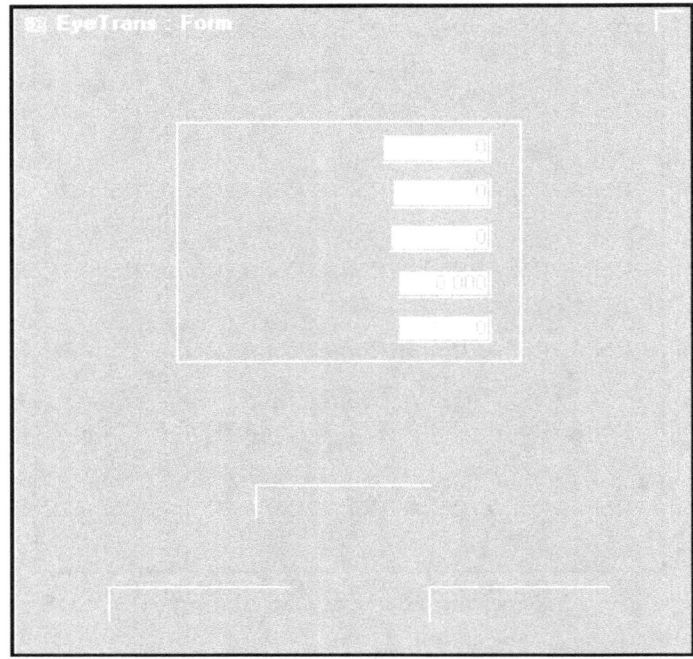

Figure 6. Program Form for Calculating EYETRANS

The analyst began by typing in the sync number corresponding to the point in the video that was approximately 3 minutes before the end of the drowsiness event (i.e., Observe Sync). Using the Observe Sync number and the sync number corresponding to the alerting event, the program calculated the time interval between the two sync numbers. The analyst then began the video from the point 3 minutes prior to the end of the drowsiness event and clicked "Start" on the program form at the same time. Whenever the analyst would see the driver transition his eyes from one location to another, the analyst would press the "t" key on the keyboard. When the analyst could not determine what was occurring in the video, he/she pressed the "x" key to exclude time in the interval. At the end of the interval, the program calculated the total number of transitions (frequency count) and divided this number by the time interval to determine the eye transition rate (i.e., the number of eye transitions per minute), or EYETRANS. When the analyst was satisfied with the output, he/she clicked "Done" and the EYETRANS analysis was saved.

EYESOFF, the proportion of time that the driver's eyes were off the road during the three-minute interval, was the fourth drowsiness/inattention measure determined by the video analyst. The process to determine EYESOFF was similar to the process used to calculate PERCLOS and

EYETRANS, the only difference being that the analyst pressed the "o" key whenever the driver's eyes were off the road. Based on the interval duration, and the total time that the driver's eyes were off the road, the EYESOFF measure was determined. Again, the EYESOFF proportion was multiplied by 100 and displayed as a percentage in the form. The form used for calculating EYESOFF was virtually identical to that used to calculate PERCLOS (Figure 5). It is important to note that EYESOFF includes the periods of time that the driver's eyes were closed or nearly closed. To determine the proportion of time that the driver glanced away from the road but did not close his eyes due to drowsiness, the PERCLOS value was subtracted from EYESOFF.

2.3   STEP 3: WRITTEN DESCRIPTION OF EVENT

Preparing a brief narrative description of each fatigue event was the third step in the data reduction/archiving process. The analyst entered the following summary information about each event on a narrative form: subject number, subject's age and gender, truck type, event date, event time, and sync number at the beginning of the event. After this information, a brief paragraph describing the event was written; a sample narrative description is presented below.

> *"The subject was extremely drowsy on this rainy afternoon as he drove in the right lane of a wet, rural, divided (median) road. Traffic was light, and visibility was limited due to the rain. His signs of drowsiness included slow blinking, multiple yawns, and slow eye closures. His driving ability was affected by his drowsiness, shown when he crossed both lane lines. The event ended on a curved roadway when he looked for something on the passenger seat."*

For each of the 1,000 events, a number of data elements were derived from the software program and from the data reduction process. A complete list and description of all the event measurements, driver demographic information, environmental conditions, and roadway factors recorded by analysts during the Task 2 data reduction process is presented in Table 3.

Table 3. List and Description of Variables for Video Analysis of 1,000 Events

Name	Description
Subject	Unique number assigned to each subject/driver.
Age	Age of the driver (years).
Gender	Gender of the driver (Female = 0; Male = 1).
Company	Company identification number (Beverage = 1; Snack = 2).
TruckTyp	L/SH truck type identification number (Panel Vans = 0; Straight Box Truck = 1; Box Truck = 2).
YrsTrucker	Number of years that the subject has been a truck driver.
YrsL/SH	Number of years the subject has been a Local/Short-Haul truck driver.
YrsLicense	Number of years that the subject has had a driver's license.
Event	Identification number for each event.
Date	The date that the event occurred.
Day	Day of week (that the event occurred) (Monday = 1; Tuesday = 2; Wednesday = 3; Thursday = 4; Friday = 5; Saturday = 6; Sunday = 7).
BeginShift	Estimated time of day that driver's shift began.
TimeDay	Time of day that the event occurred (given in 24-hr and in 12-hr time).
TimeDuty	Estimated amount of time (hours and minutes) from the start of the driver's shift until the drowsy event occurred.
SlpQual	A subjective rating the driver gave of his/her sleep from the previous night (rating was given the next morning) (Terrible = 1; Fair = 3; Excellent = 5; there are not descriptions assigned to the ratings of 2 and 4, although the driver was allowed to give any number between 1 and 5).
TimeBed	The number of hours the driver spent in bed the previous night.
AssuSleep	Assumed Sleep as calculated by the Sleepwatch program; given the time the driver went to bed (SleepTime) and the time he got out of bed (WakeTime), Sleepwatch hypothesizes when the driver actually fell asleep and when he actually woke up; the difference between these is Assumed Sleep.
ActSleep	Actual Sleep as calculated by the Sleepwatch program; if the Actiwatch determines the driver to be awake during the night (tossing and turning, etc.), these times are subtracted from the Assumed Sleep to arrive at Actual Sleep.
SleepEff	Sleep Efficiency measure from the Sleepwatch program, derived by dividing Actual Sleep by Time in Bed and multiplying by 100 (on a scale from 1 to 100).
ObsSync	Sync number that is approximately 3 minutes from drowsiness event end point or SyncEnd.
SyncBeg	Beginning sync number of the drowsiness event.
SyncEnd	Sync number at the end of the drowsiness event (T=0).
Duration	Total time length of the drowsiness event (event start point to end point).
OBSERV	Analyst's rating of driver drowsiness for the event; drowsiness scale ranges from 1 (not drowsy) to 5 (extremely drowsy).
PERCLOS	Time that eyes are closed or nearly closed (80–100% closed), divided by the three-minute measurement interval prior to the event end point; values are given in proportion and percentage (x100).
EYETRANS	Number of eye transitions, from one major area to another, divided by the three-minute measurement interval prior to the event end point.
EYESOFF	Total time eyes were off the road divided by the three-minute measurement interval prior to the event's end point; includes all values of PERCLOS; can subtract out PERCLOS value to obtain EYESOFF without drowsiness; values are given in proportion and percentage (x100).
LatAccel	Peak lateral acceleration (g) calculated over an interval beginning 10 seconds before the beginning of the event to the end of the event.
LongAccel	Peak longitudinal acceleration (g) calculated over an interval beginning 10 seconds before the beginning of the event to the end of the event.

Name	Description
Velocity	Mean velocity (mph) calculated over an interval beginning 10 seconds before the beginning of the event to the end of the event.
NormIllu	Mean normalized illumination sensor value; scale from 0 (complete darkness) to 1 (bright light).
Density	Density of surrounding traffic assessed in terms of level-of-service (LOS) (LOS A = 0; LOS B = 1; LOS C = 2; LOS D = 3; LOS E = 4; LOS F = 5; Not Applicable = 6).
NumLanes	Number of lanes of roadway going in same direction as truck.
DrivLane	Lane that the driver was in at the end of the event (Not Applicable = 0; Right Lane = 1; Middle Lane = 2; Left Lane = 3; Shoulder = 4; Entrance/Exit Ramp = 5; Other = 6).
RoadType	Type of roadway (Parking Lot/Loading Area = 0; Alley Way = 1; One Way Road = 2; Rural Undivided = 3; Rural Divided by Median = 4; Rural Divided by Lane = 5; Urban Undivided = 6; Urban Divided by Median = 7; Urban Divided by Lane = 8; Other = 9).
RoadGeom	Geometry of the roadway (Straightaway = 0; Curve = 1; Intersection on Straightaway = 2; Intersection on Curve = 3; Loading Area = 4; Merge Lane from Right = 5; Merge Lane from Left = 6; Other = 7).
RoadCond	Condition of the roadway (Dry = 0; Wet = 1; Icy/Snow = 2; Gravel/Sand on Road = 3; Gravel Road = 4; Other = 5).
Weather	Weather conditions (Clear/Dry = 1; Drizzle = 2; Hard Rain = 3; Light Snow = 4; Hard Snow = 5; Sleet = 6; Other = 7; Cloudy = 8).
Visibility	Visibility outside of vehicle (Unlimited = 1; Rain = 2; Snow = 3; Fog = 4; Darkness = 5; Glare from Sun = 6; Glare from Headlights = 7; Twilight = 8; Other = 9).
Illum	Illumination outside of vehicle (Dawn = 1; Daylight = 2; Dusk = 3; Night = 4; Other = 5).

2.4   DATA ANALYSIS

This section describes the statistical techniques that were used to analyze the data obtained during the data reduction/archiving process.

2.4.1   Analysis of Variance

In statistics, analysis of variance (ANOVA) is a technique to assess how several nominal independent variables affect a continuous dependent variable. ANOVA is usually employed in comparisons involving several population means. One-way ANOVA refers to the simplest case of ANOVA, which involves a comparison of population means between two groups.

As an example, suppose researchers are interested in investigating the driver characteristics that significantly affect driver drowsiness. Specifically, they would like to compare the mean values of age in two groups of drivers—those that experience high levels of drowsiness while driving and those that experience low levels of on-the-job drowsiness. An ANOVA tests the following hypothesis in Figure 7.

$$H_0: \mu Age(High) = \mu Age(Low)$$
$$H_1: \mu Age(High) \neq \mu Age(Low)$$

Figure 7.

The null hypothesis is that the mean age in the High Fatigue group of drivers is equal to the mean age in the Low Fatigue group of drivers. The alternative hypothesis is that the average ages of the High Fatigue and Low Fatigue groups are not equal. If the calculated F-statistic is greater than the critical value at a 0.05 significance level (i.e., $\alpha = 0.05$), then we can reject the null hypothesis H_0 and conclude that the mean values of age in the High Fatigue and Low Fatigue driver groups are significantly different, thereby suggesting that age is a contributing factor to driver drowsiness.

2.4.2 Discriminant Analysis

A linear discriminant function is a statistical method designed to classify an observation into one of several categories. For this study, the L/SH fatigue data were used to develop a discriminant function that predicts whether a driver is likely to belong to a "High Fatigue" or a "Low Fatigue" group based on such factors as age, driving experience, and sleep habits. A discriminant function is relatively simple (linear), combines multivariate measurements (e.g., driver characteristics) into a single value called the discriminant score, and allows classification of observations into a series of categories with minimum misclassification. Thus, the goal of the discriminant analysis is to predict a categorical response (whether a driver will experience high or low levels of fatigue) based on a set of continuous predictor variables.

2.4.3 Contingency Table Analysis

Contingency table analysis is a statistical method that applies to multivariate but discrete data, distributed into tables. With contingency tables, relationships between a categorical response (Fatigue vs. Baseline) and categorical predictor variables are examined. The following variables from Table 3 were evaluated:

- Time of Day (grouped in eight 3-hour segments).

- Traffic Density (Density).

- Lane that the Driver Occupied (DrivLane).

- Type of Roadway (RoadType).

- Road Geometry (RoadGeom).

- Road Condition (RoadCond).

- Weather Conditions (Weather).

- Visibility Outside the Vehicle (Visibility).

- Lighting Conditions Outside the Vehicle (Illum).

When each sampled event is classified by one or more characteristics, the total number of events with the same characteristics make up the cell frequencies of a contingency table. The essence of a statistical analysis of contingency table data is, then, the comparison of the observed values to theoretically generated expected values. As an example, consider whether there is a relationship between fatigued driving and traffic density. A contingency table to explore such a relationship would look like Table 4 below.

Table 4. Sample Contingency Table

Event	Traffic Density LOS A	Traffic Density LOS B	Traffic Density LOS C	Traffic Density LOS D	Traffic Density LOS E	Traffic Density LOS F	Total
Fatigue	f_{11}	f_{12}	f_{13}	f_{14}	f_{15}	f_{16}	**607**
Baseline	f_{21}	f_{22}	f_{23}	f_{24}	f_{25}	f_{26}	**393**
Total	–	–	–	–	–	–	**1,000**

The hypothesis being tested is:

- H_0: Traffic density and drowsiness are independent.

- H_1: There is an association between traffic density and drowsiness.

Association between traffic density and drowsiness can be measured using the Pearson chi-square statistic and the likelihood ratio chi-square statistic.

2.4.4   Stepwise Linear Regression

Stepwise linear regression was conducted to identify the independent variables that significantly influence differences in the three measurements of drowsiness and inattention: PERCLOS, EYETRANS, and EYESOFF. The problem of deciding which of the variables in Table 3 may affect driver fatigue and inattention is difficult. Stepwise regression is a screening procedure that provides a systematic approach to building a model with a potentially large number of predictor variables.

Basically, the stepwise regression procedure begins by specifying the response variable (e.g., PERCLOS) and a complete set of potentially significant independent variables. The set of independent variables can contain continuous or categorical variables as well as any interaction terms that might be important information contributors. The independent variable that produces the largest (absolute) t value is selected and retained, and the software package then searches through the remaining variables for the best two-variable model. This forward selection process continues until no further independent variables can be found that yield significant t values in the presence of the variables already in the model. The result is a model containing only the main effects with t values that are significant at the $\alpha = 0.05$ level (or whatever other significance level is desired). Thus, the factors having the most important impact on driver fatigue are identified.

2.4.5   Logistic Regression

The data in this study were analyzed using logistic regression, a mathematical modeling approach that can be used to describe the relationship of several independent or predictor variables to a binary or dichotomous dependent variable (in this case, fatigue vs. baseline event).

The logistic regression model is shown below in Figure 8:

$$PR(Fatigue) = \frac{1}{1+e^{-z}}$$

Where $z = \beta_0 + \beta_1 X_1 + \beta_2 X_2 + \ldots\ldots + \beta_n X_n$
(n = number of independent or predictor variables)
and β is the coefficient of the predictor variable X

Figure 8. Logistic Regression Model

The logistic regression equation shows that the probability of fatigue is equal to 1 divided by the sum of 1 plus e to the power negative z, where z is equal to the sum of beta subscript zero plus beta subscript 1 times X subscript 1 plus beta subscript 2 times X subscript 2, and the sum continues up to beta subscript n times X subscript n (n is the number of predictor variables in the model).

The estimated model was used to predict the probability of a particular response, in this case a drowsy-driving event, based on a set of predictor variables chosen from Table 3. As in any regression model, the regression coefficients β_i in the logistic model play an important role in providing information about the relationships of the predictor variables in the model to the dependent variable. For the logistic model, quantification of these relationships involves a parameter called the odds ratio. The odds of a fatigue event occurring are defined and shown in Figure 9:

$$\frac{PR(Fatigue)}{PR(No\ Fatigue)} = e^{\beta_0 + \beta_1 X_1 + \beta_2 X_2 + \ldots\ldots + \beta_n X_n} = e^{\beta_0}\ e^{\beta_1 X_1}\ \beta_2 X_2 + \ldots\ldots\ e^{\beta_n X_n}$$

Figure 9. Drowsy-Driving Event based on a Set of Predictor Variables

The equation for the odds of a fatigue event is expressed as follows: The quotient of the probability of fatigue divided by the probability of no fatigue equals the exponentiated sum of beta subscript zero plus beta subscript 1 times X subscript 1 plus beta subscript 2 times X subscript 2 ad infinitum up to beta subscript n times X subscript n. This, in turn, equals the exponent of the product of beta subscript zero multiplied by the exponent of the product of beta subscript 1 times X subscript 1, with the multiplication continuing up to the exponent of the product of beta subscript n times X subscript n.

Logistic regression determines the *beta* coefficients that make the observed outcome (fatigue or non-fatigue event) most "likely" using the maximum likelihood method. Maximum likelihood estimates are those which, generally speaking, ascribe the highest likelihood to the observed data. Thus, the application of the logistic regression model yields a set of estimated odds ratios, determined from the *beta* coefficients, which are useful and readily interpretable measures of association. The results of a logistic regression model yield a set of p-values for each *beta* coefficient. Each p-value tests the null hypothesis that the adjusted odds ratio for that X variable equals 1.0 in the overall population. In other words, the null hypothesis being tested is that there is no association between the X variable and the occurrence of driver fatigue, after adjusting for all other X variables.

Logistic regression analysis complemented the stepwise linear regression technique described in the previous section. Whereas stepwise linear regression identifies the factors that significantly influence driver fatigue (as measured by PERCLOS), logistic models were developed to investigate the driver, roadway, and environmental factors that increase the likelihood of occurrence of fatigued or drowsy driving episodes.

The detailed video reduction/archiving of 1,000 events provided the data used in the analyses, and statistical models were developed for the data stratified by fatigue severity, as indicated by the Observer Rating of Drowsiness assigned to each event. Thus, separate analyses were performed for:

- All 1,000 fatigue and baseline events.

- ORD 4 and ORD 5 vs. matched baseline events.

- ORD 2 and ORD 3 vs. matched baseline events.

3. RESULTS

3.1 CHARACTERIZATION OF LOCAL/SHORT-HAUL DRIVER FATIGUE

Analysts reviewed the entire L/SH video library and identified all episodes of fatigue and drowsiness for the 41 drivers. (Note: 42 drivers participated in the L/SH field study; however, there were no usable data for subject number 1 due to a data acquisition malfunction.) For each drowsiness event, analysts recorded the duration and assigned an ORD based on a scale of 2 (slightly drowsy) to 5 (extremely drowsy). An ORD value of 1 is, by definition, considered to be a baseline, or non-drowsiness, event.

A total of 2,745 fatigue or drowsy events were identified in approximately 900 total hours of driving. Thus, the rate of drowsy occurrences for all drivers combined was 3.1 events per hour of driving. On a per-driver basis, the drowsiness rate varied from 0 to 9.3 events per hour. The frequency distribution by ORD rating and the event duration from drowsiness onset to the alerting activity (the activity that "snaps" the driver out of his drowsy state) are summarized in Table 5. As expected, given how ORD ratings are determined, the longer a drowsy event lasts, the more severe it is in terms of ORD.

Table 5. Distribution of Frequency and Duration of Fatigue Events by ORD

Event	Number of Occurrences	Duration (seconds) Mean	Duration (seconds) Minimum	Duration (seconds) Maximum
ORD 2 (Slightly Drowsy)	1,636	13.4	0.4	330.0
ORD 3 (Moderately Drowsy)	824	61.4	1.4	557.2
ORD 4 (Very Drowsy)	160	102.0	11.3	441.6
ORD 5 (Extremely Drowsy)	125	179.4	15.2	837.0
All Events	**2,745**	**40.5**	**0.4**	**837.0**

Table 6 summarizes the results of the video data review by driver. It clearly illustrates the considerable subject-to-subject variation in drowsiness behavior among the 41 L/SH drivers. Five drivers (subjects 2, 4, 5, 9, and 41) never, or almost never, exhibited signs of drowsiness while driving their trucks; on the other hand, driver number 18 had 224 instances of drowsiness, 70 more than any other driver. The average event duration ranged from 5 seconds (driver 18) to almost 2 minutes (driver 7). Another interesting descriptive measure of driver drowsiness is the percentage of total driving hours that each driver was drowsy or fatigued. For all drivers collectively, almost 31 hours, or 3.5 percent of overall driving time, were spent in being drowsy. The breakdown for each driver is shown in Figure 10. And finally, the distribution of drowsiness events by ORD for each driver is presented in Figure 11 through Figure 18.

Table 6. Fatigue Analysis Results Summary by Driver

Driver	Total Driving Time (hr)	Number of Events	Number of Events/Hr	Total Fatigue Duration (sec)	Mean Event Duration (sec)	Fatigue % of Driving Time
2	19	1	0.1	7.6	7.6	0.0
3	17	24	1.4	188.6	7.86	0.3
4	14	2	0.1	15.7	7.85	0.0
5	8	0	0.0	0.0	—	0.0
6	22	41	1.9	4,267.5	104.08	5.4
7	37	154	4.2	17,927.5	116.41	13.5
8	11	19	1.7	898.1	47.27	2.3
9	13	1	0.1	5.0	5.0	0.0
10	22	41	1.9	1,139.8	27.80	1.4
11	18	21	1.2	548.4	26.11	0.8
12	22	112	5.1	3,431.0	30.63	4.3
13	31	115	3.7	9,043.3	78.64	8.1
14	48	40	0.8	326.0	8.15	0.2
15	15	59	3.9	3,706.3	62.82	6.9
16	50	52	1.0	1,038.6	19.97	0.6
17	28	136	4.9	11,369.7	83.60	11.3
18	41	224	5.5	1,236.0	5.52	0.8
19	23	106	4.6	2,989.4	28.20	3.6
20	26	119	4.6	1,786.4	15.01	1.9
21	30	120	4.0	4,266.5	35.55	4.0
22	24	143	6.0	2,659.0	18.59	3.1
23	21	31	1.5	1,232.6	39.76	1.6
24	20	83	4.2	5,444.2	65.59	7.6
25	19	87	4.6	6,189.1	71.14	9.0
26	16	69	4.3	555.5	8.05	1.0
27	23	42	1.8	870.2	20.72	1.1
28	16	68	4.3	964.0	14.18	1.7
29	20	92	4.6	2,613.6	28.41	3.6
30	18	42	2.3	1,538.5	36.63	2.4
40	13	30	2.3	792.2	26.41	1.7
41	12	1	0.1	5.9	5.90	0.0
42	17	22	1.3	299.6	13.62	0.5
43	12	18	1.5	152.1	8.45	0.4
44	11	102	9.3	3,356.5	32.91	8.5
45	21	132	6.3	8,600.2	65.15	11.4
46	18	27	1.5	1,058.4	39.20	1.6
47	29	75	2.6	4,039.8	53.86	3.9
48	13	71	5.5	1,513.6	21.32	3.2
49	33	106	3.2	1,991.9	18.79	1.7
50	20	47	2.4	1,450.5	30.86	2.0
51	18	70	3.9	1,697.1	24.24	2.6
ALL	889	2,745	3.1	111,215.9	40.52	3.5

Figure 10 presents a bar chart of the proportion of the driving time in which the drivers were drowsy or fatigued. There is one bar corresponding to each of the 41 drivers in the study. The driver number is shown along the x-axis, and the y-axis is the percent of total driving hours. The chart shows that drivers 2, 4, 5, 9, and 41 were drowsy for 0 percent of total driving hours and that drivers 7, 17, and 45 experienced drowsiness during 13.5, 11.3, and 11.4 percent of their driving hours, respectively. All other drivers ranged from 0.3 to 9 percent.

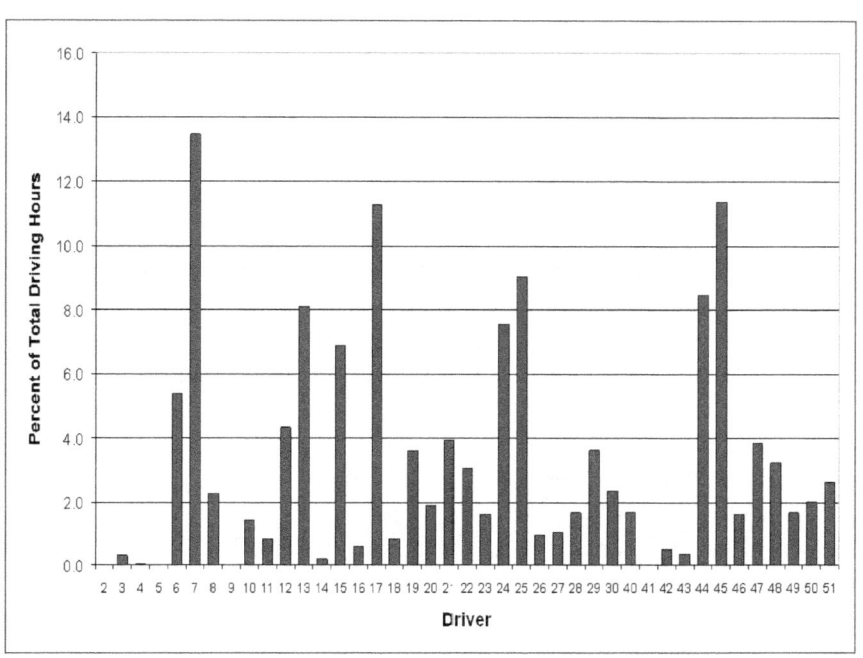

Figure 10. Proportion of Drowsy Driving for Each L/SH Driver

Figure 11 through Figure 18 are all bar graphs showing the number of drowsiness events (along the y-axis) experienced by each driver (on the x-axis); five drivers are presented on each chart. Figure 11, showing drivers 2 through 7, presents the following data: Driver 2 experienced one ORD 2 event; driver 3 experienced 24 ORD 2 events; driver 4 experienced two ORD 2 events; driver 6 experienced 16 ORD 2 events, 23 ORD 3 events, and two ORD 4 events; and driver 7 experienced 40 ORD 2 events, 107 ORD 3 events, and seven ORD 4 events.

Figure 12, for drivers 8 through 12, presents the following results: Driver 8 was observed to have 12 ORD 2 events and seven ORD 3 events; driver 9 was observed to have one ORD 2 event; driver 10 was observed to have 38 ORD 2 events and three ORD 3 events; driver 11 was observed to have nine ORD 2 events and 12 ORD 3 events; and driver 12 was observed to have 64 ORD 2 events, 34 ORD 3 events, 13 ORD 4 events, and one ORD 5 event.

Figure 13 shows the following data for drivers 13 through 17: Driver 13 experienced 53 ORD 2 events, 40 ORD 3 events, four ORD 4 events, and 18 ORD 5 events; driver 14 experienced 39 ORD 2 events and one ORD 3 event; driver 15 experienced 18 ORD 2 events, 17 ORD 3 events, and 24 ORD 4 events; driver 16 experienced 32 ORD 2 events and 20 ORD 3 events; and driver 17 experienced 50 ORD 2 events, 67 ORD 3 events, 15 ORD 4 events, and four ORD 5 events.

Figure 14 presents the following data for drivers 18 through 22: Driver 18 experienced 221 ORD 2 events and three ORD 3 events; driver 19 experienced 60 ORD 2 events, 39 ORD 3 events, five ORD 4 events, and two ORD 5 events; driver 20 experienced 86 ORD 2 events, 27 ORD 3 events, one ORD 4 events, and five ORD 5 events; driver 21 experienced 81 ORD 2 events, 22 ORD 3 events, five ORD 4 events, and 12 ORD 5 events; and driver 22 experienced 111 ORD 2 events, 28 ORD 3 events, and four ORD 4 events.

Figure 15 presents results for drivers 23 through 27. This chart shows that: Driver 23 was observed to have 17 ORD 2 events, 11 ORD 3 events, one ORD 4 event, and two ORD 5 events; driver 24 was observed to have five ORD 2 events, 66 ORD 3 events, and 12 ORD 4 events; driver 25 was observed to have 35 ORD 2 events, 20 ORD 3 events, 11 ORD 4 events, and 21 ORD 5 events; driver 26 was observed to have 68 ORD 2 events and one ORD 3 event; and driver 27 was observed to have 38 ORD 2 events, one ORD 3 event, and three ORD 5 events.

Figure 16 shows results for drivers 28 through 41. Driver 28 experienced 50 ORD 2 events, 16 ORD 3 events, one ORD 4 event, and one ORD 5 event; driver 29 experienced 56 ORD 2 events, 29 ORD 3 events, and 7 ORD 4 events; driver 30 experienced 26 ORD 2 events, 11 ORD 3 events, one ORD 4 event, and four ORD 5 events; driver 40 experienced 26 ORD 2 events, two ORD 3 events, one ORD 4 event, and one ORD 5 event; and driver 41 experienced one ORD 2 event.

Figure 17 presents the following results for drivers 42 through 46: Driver 42 was observed to have 19 ORD 2 events and three ORD 3 events; driver 43 was observed to have 18 ORD 2 events; driver 44 was observed to have 61 ORD 2 events, 28 ORD 3 events, six ORD 4 events, and seven ORD 5 events; driver 45 was observed to have 45 ORD 2 events, 44 ORD 3 events, 23 ORD 4 events, and 20 ORD 5 events; and driver 46 was observed to have 10 ORD 2 events, 12 ORD 3 events, one ORD 4 event, and four ORD 5 events.

Figure 18 shows the following data for drivers 47 through 51: Driver 47 experienced 27 ORD 2 events, 39 ORD 3 events, four ORD 4 events, and five ORD 5 events; driver 48 experienced 53 ORD 2 events and 18 ORD 3 events; driver 49 experienced 69 ORD 2 events, 24 ORD 3 events, five ORD 4 events, and eight ORD 5 events; driver 50 experienced 11 ORD 2 events, 24 ORD 3 events, seven ORD 4 events, and five ORD 5 events; and driver 51 experienced 43 ORD 2 events, 25 ORD 3 events, and two ORD 5 events.

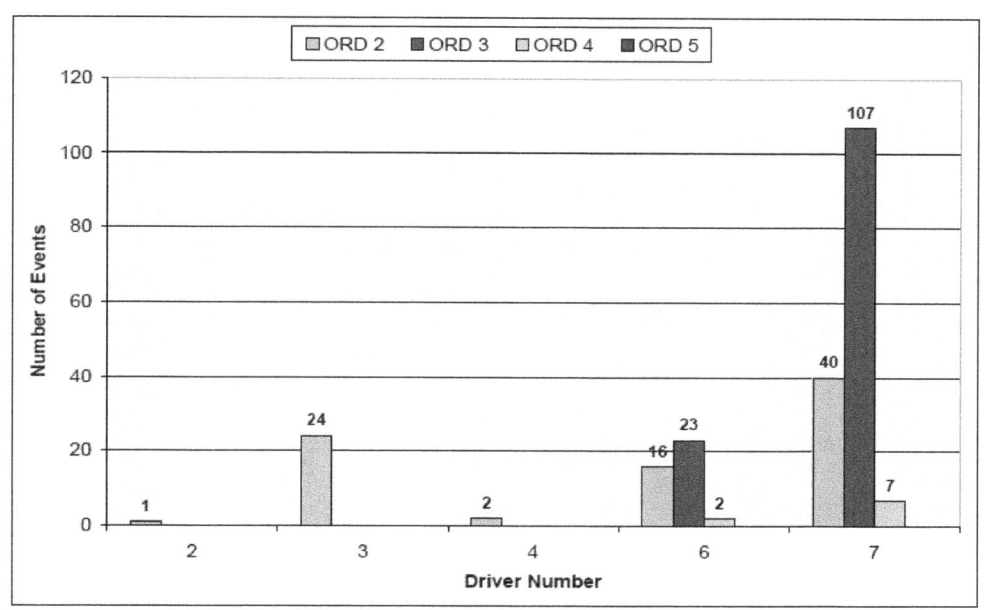

Figure 11. Drowsiness Events as a Function of ORD Level for Drivers 2–7

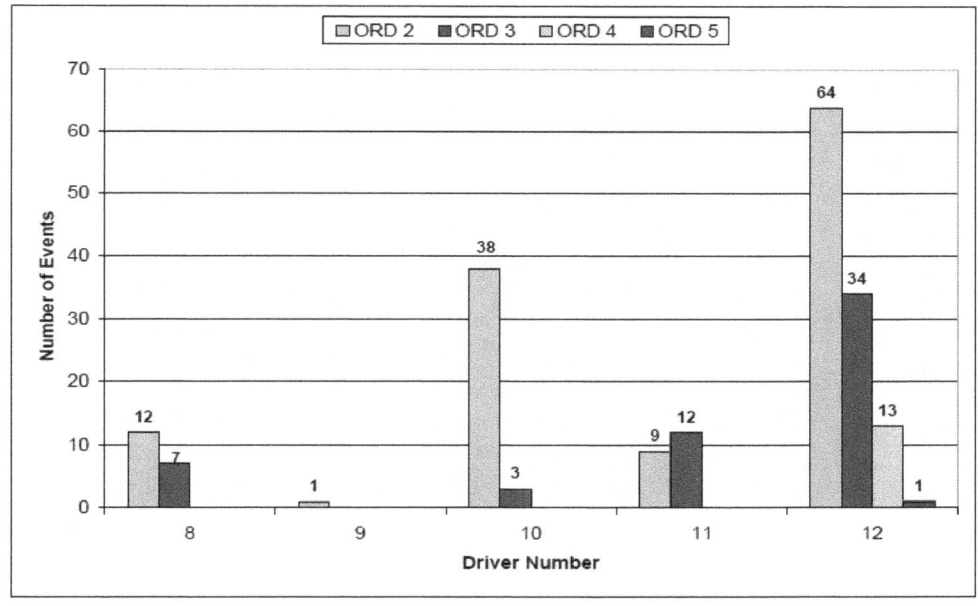

Figure 12. Drowsiness Events as a Function of ORD Level for Drivers 8–12

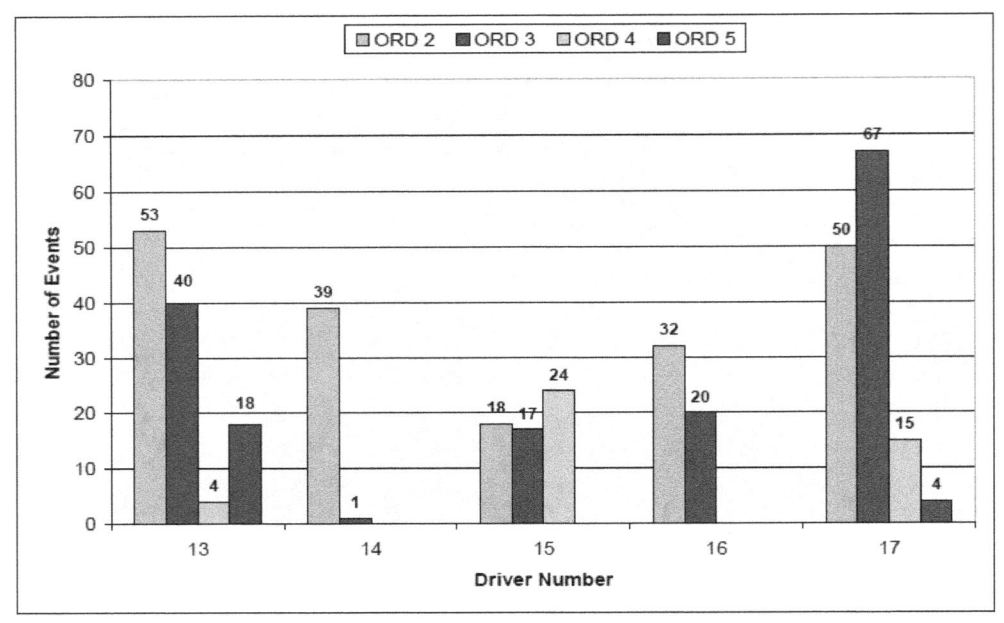

Figure 13. Drowsiness Events as a Function of ORD Level for Drivers 13–17

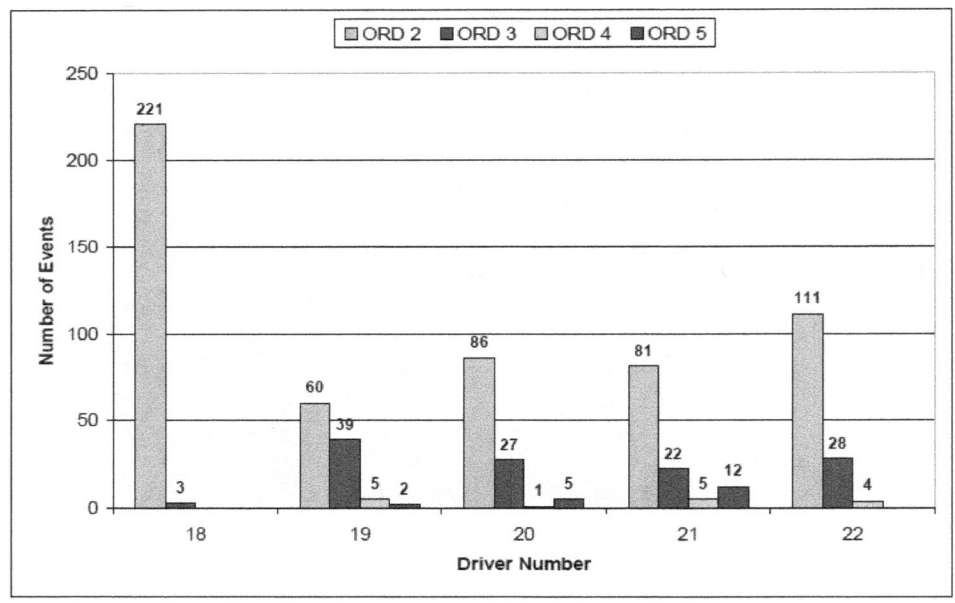

Figure 14. Drowsiness Events as a Function of ORD Level for Drivers 18–22

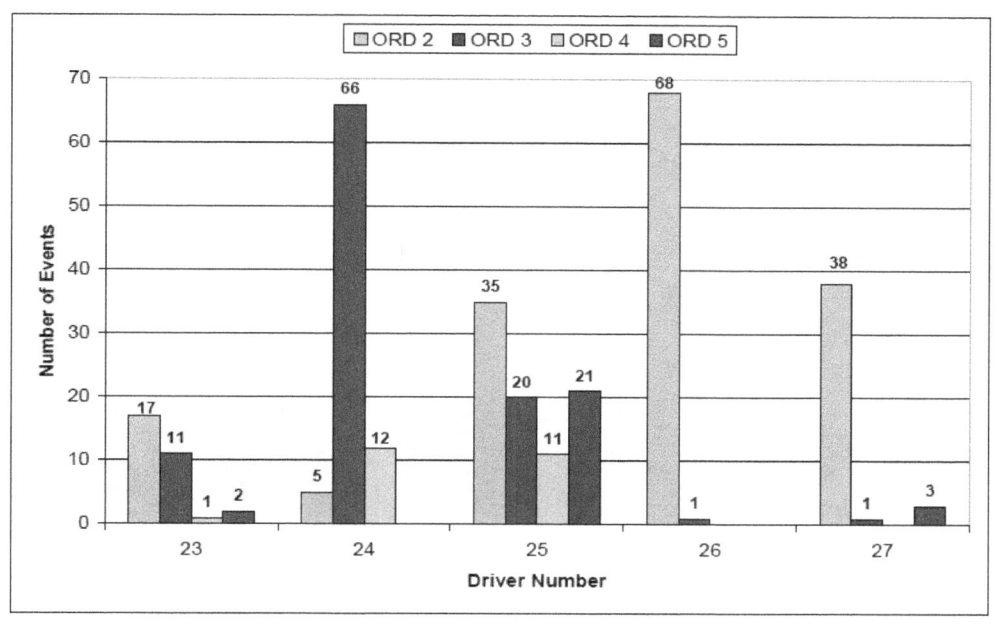

Figure 15. Drowsiness Events as a Function of ORD Level for Drivers 23–27

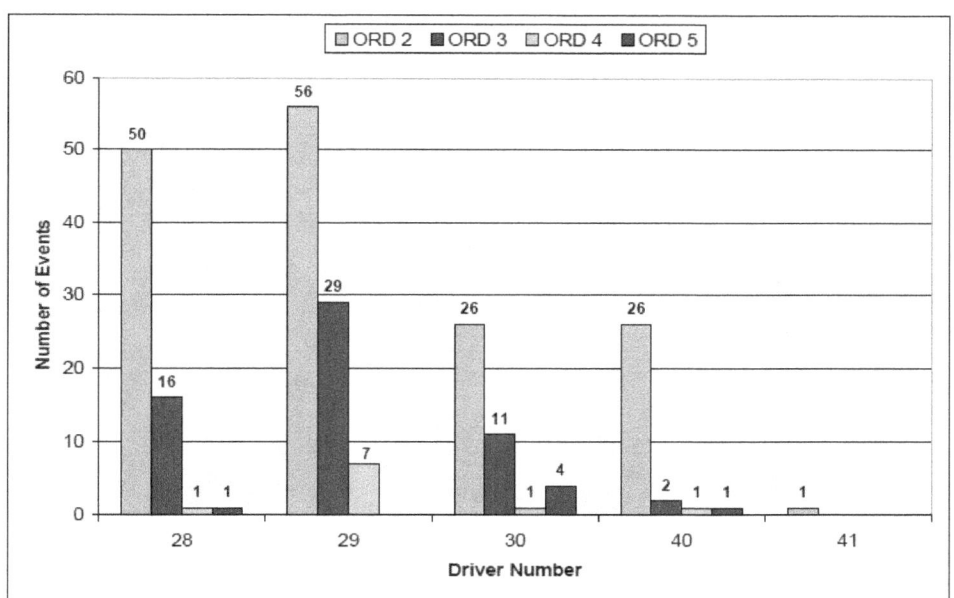

Figure 16. Drowsiness Events as a Function of ORD Level for Drivers 28–41

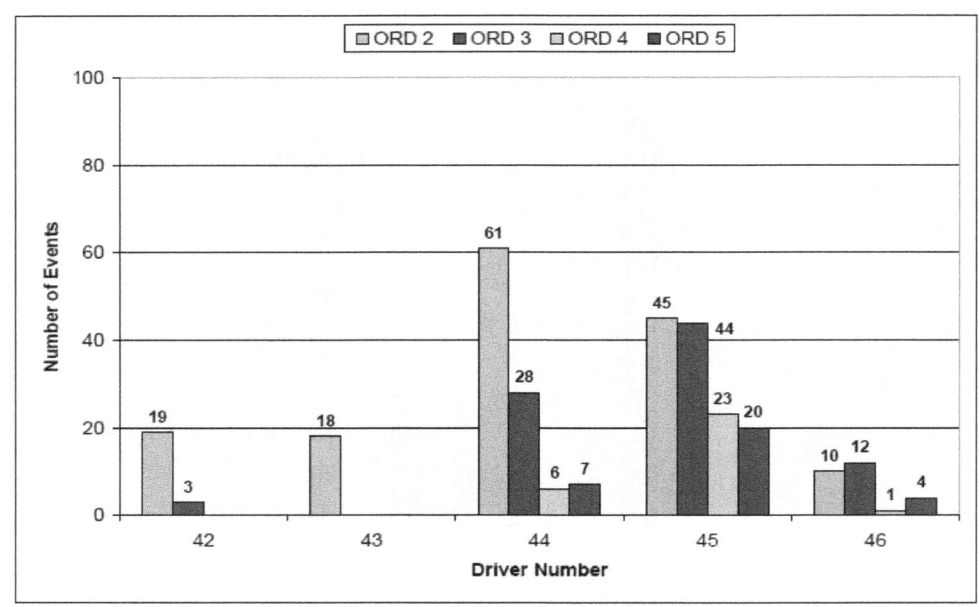

Figure 17. Drowsiness Events as a Function of ORD Level for Drivers 42–46

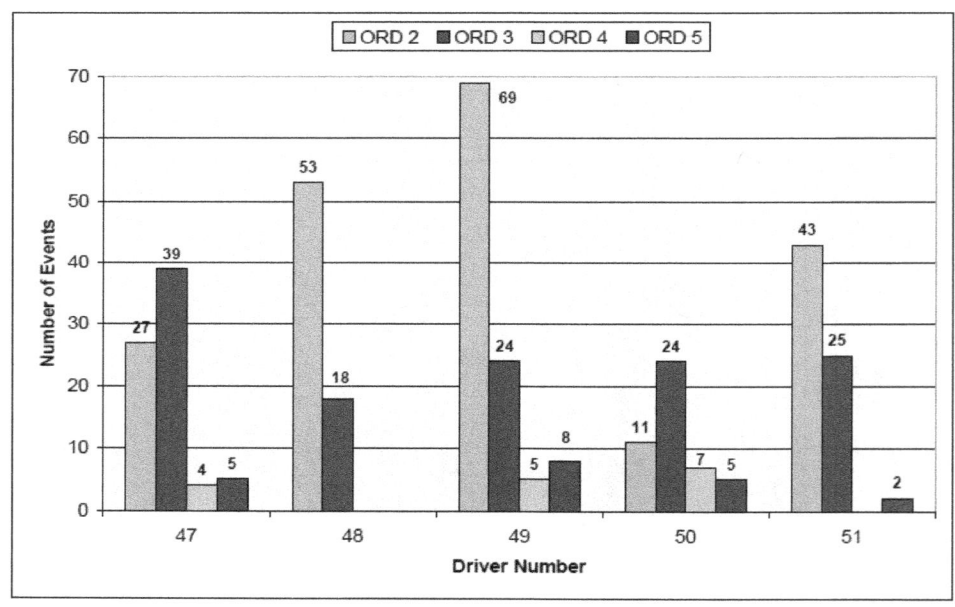

Figure 18. Drowsiness Events as a Function of ORD Level for Drivers 47–51

In addition to establishing the frequency, duration, and severity of all drowsy events, video analysts also determined the alerting activity that appeared to bring the driver out of his drowsy state and restore his full attention to the driving task. In a study examining the impact of sleepiness and drowsiness on motor vehicle crashes, researchers at the University of North Carolina Highway Research Center asked drivers what, if anything, they did to stay awake and alert when they found themselves feeling drowsy while driving (Stutts, Wilkins, & Vaughn, 1999). The most common strategy, cited by nearly half of all drivers in the study, was to open windows or adjust the air conditioner or heater to let in fresh air and reduce the temperature.

Other frequently cited countermeasure strategies for staying awake and alert while driving included listening to the radio or CD player (32 percent of respondents), eating or drinking (24 percent), and talking to a passenger (4 percent). In addition, approximately 14 percent of the respondents stated that they would stop to rest or take a nap, 24 percent would stop to get something to eat or drink, and 16 percent would stop to stretch, exercise, or walk around.

The distribution of observed alerting events from this study of L/SH drivers is shown in Figure 19. This is a bar graph showing the number of alerting events along the vertical axis and the categories or types of alerting activities along the horizontal axis. In some cases, specific activities were grouped into higher-level categories; hence, for example, a biomechanical alerting event includes activities such as tuning the radio, adjusting the seat or visor, and shifting or moving around in the seat. Similarly, grooming includes biting fingernails, scratching the head, and rubbing the face, and performing a driving task involves things such as changing lanes, making a turn, merging onto another road, and slowing down for traffic ahead. Figure 19 shows that 627 drowsy events, or 21 percent of the overall total, ended with no obvious or clearly discernible alerting activity. By far the most frequent alerting event, ending more than 28 percent of all drowsy episodes, was looking outside at a passing vehicle or simply scanning the surrounding environment. Looking outside is followed by performing a driving task (12.0 percent), a biomechanical activity (8.7 percent), stopping at a traffic light or stop sign (5.8 percent), or talking to a passenger (4.6 percent) as frequently observed activities that alert a driver after a period of drowsiness. Summarizing the results shown in Figure 19, the numbers and types of alerting activities are as follows: 627 No Obvious Activity, 90 Eating/Drinking, 50 Smoking, 125 Talking to a Passenger, 774 Looking Outside, 147 Looking Inside the Cab, 239 Biomechanical, 133 Grooming, 158 Stopping at a Traffic Light, 330 Executing a Driving Task, and 3 Stopping to Rest.

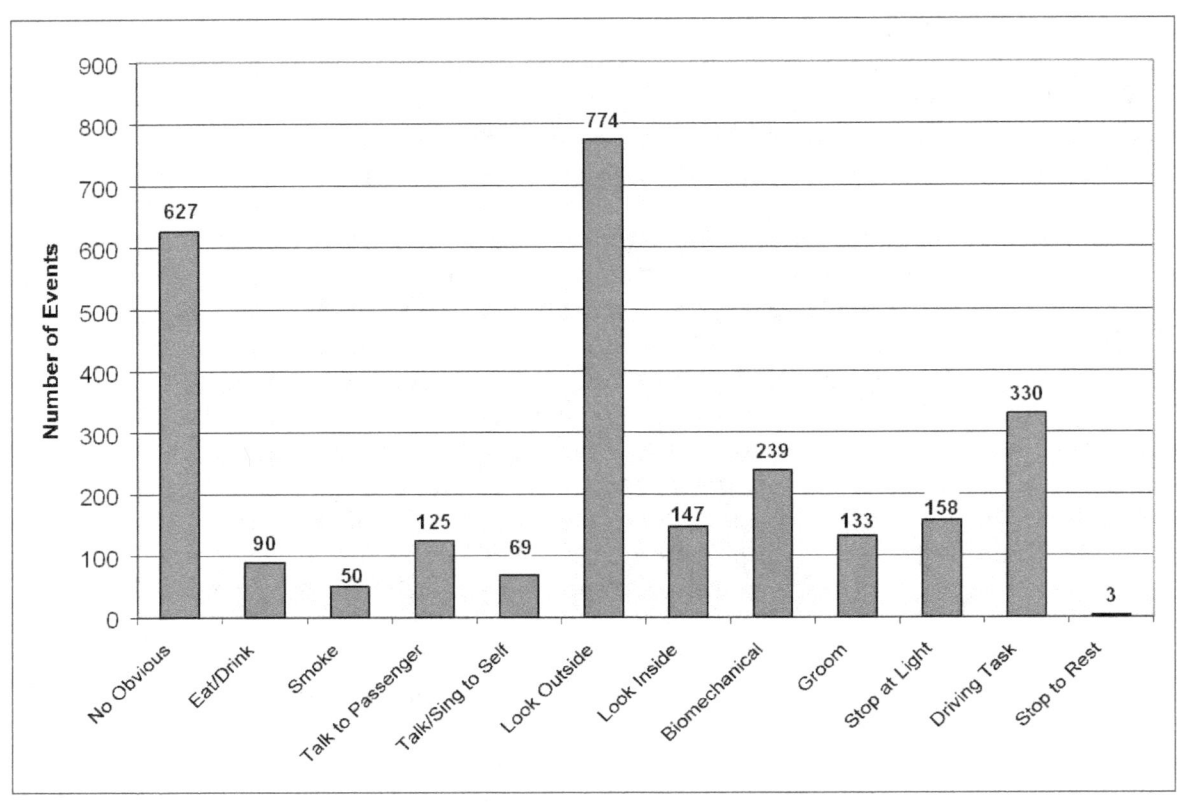

Figure 19. Activities Used by Drivers to Stop Drowsiness

While drivers may list a number of countermeasure activities they would employ to stay awake and alert while driving (Stutts et al., 1999), this study of naturalistic driving shows that actual behavior in response to fatigue and drowsiness can be quite different. Rather than adopting a voluntary and active response to counteract drowsiness (opening windows, adjusting the climate control and audio settings, drinking caffeinated beverages), these data showed that oftentimes simply responding to a change in the driving environment (making a turn, slowing or stopping in traffic, or looking out the window at a passing vehicle) is what alerts a driver and ends his drowsiness. Also, a fairly common strategy for staying awake and alert cited in the North Carolina study (Stutts et al., 1999) was to stop and take a break from driving. However, this study of L/SH drivers found this strategy to be almost nonexistent. Some of these differences could be explained by the dissimilar driving populations in the two studies; this study employed commercial L/SH drivers who operate under greater schedule pressure than the general driving population. Also, it is important to keep in mind that the results shown in Figure 19 are based on subjective observations made by the video analysts. Nevertheless, comparing the results from this study with the data from the North Carolina study points out some important differences in drivers' stated preferences vs. their revealed preferences (actual behavior).

The descriptive statistics presented in this section show that drivers experience widely varying levels of drowsiness throughout their workdays. The total number and duration of fatigue events experienced by a driver does not provide an accurate or complete indication of the level of fatigue he experiences while driving. A simple frequency count does not include the severity of drowsiness (for example, a short yawn vs. multiple complete eye closures), nor does it take into account the amount of driving done by each driver. The data shown in Figure 10 account for overall driving hours but do not capture fatigue severity. Therefore, a measure of fatigue called the Fatigue Index was developed for each driver in this study. The Fatigue Index accounts for the frequency of occurrence of drowsy episodes, normalized by total driving time, as well as the severity of the fatigue event. It is defined as the sum of the ORD ratings for all fatigue events divided by the total number of hours of driving data analyzed. The Fatigue Index for each driver in the L/SH study is pictured in Figure 20. This bar chart shows the Fatigue Index on the vertical axis for each driver along the x-axis. The lowest values of fatigue index are 0.11 for driver 2, 0 for driver 5, 0.15 for driver 9, and 0.17 for driver 41. They range up to the highest values of 24.09 and 19.71 for drivers 44 and 45, respectively. All other drivers have Fatigue Index values of less than 15. The median value of the Fatigue Index for all 41 drivers is 7.35; this value was used as a cut-point for placing the drivers in one of two groups. Drivers with a Fatigue Index higher than the median value are categorized as "High Fatigue" drivers, while those with a Fatigue Index less than or equal to the median value are designated "Low Fatigue" drivers.

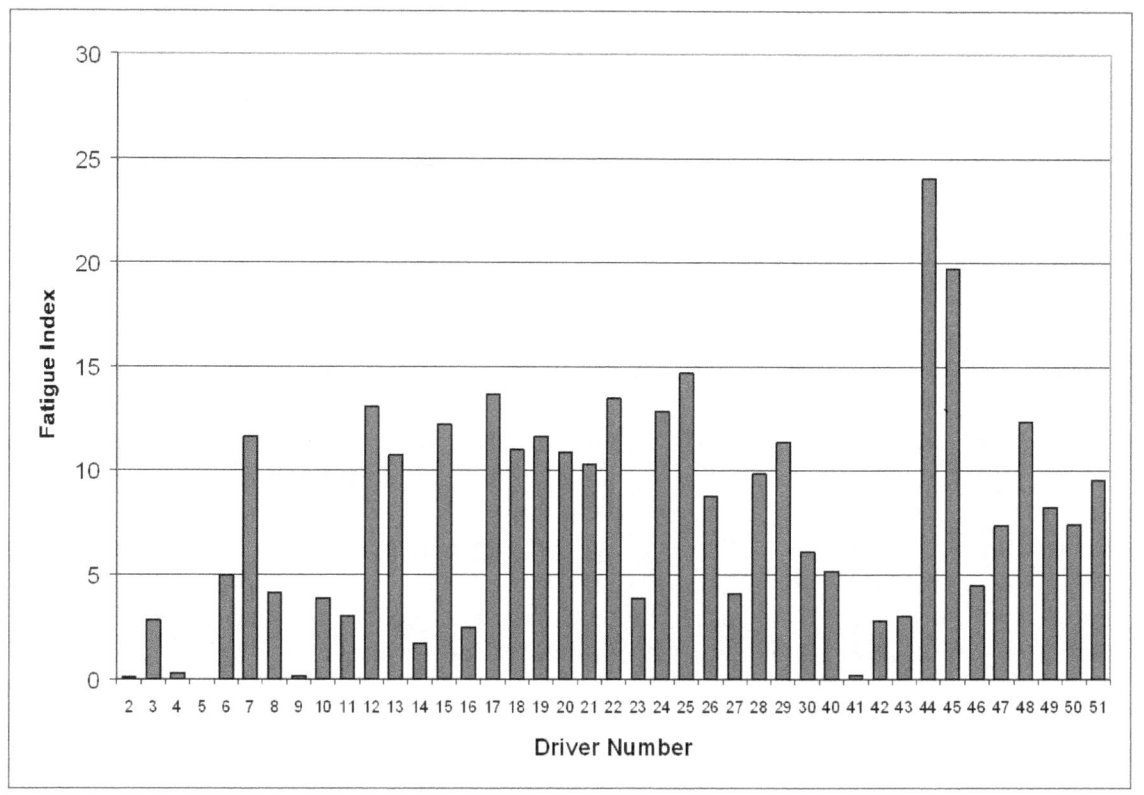

Figure 20. Fatigue Index for Each L/SH Driver

Statistical analyses were conducted using the driver as the unit of observation to identify relationships between fatigue/drowsiness and various driver characteristics. The researchers collected demographic data for each driver during the L/SH field study; Table 7 shows the driver characteristics that were used in the analyses.

Table 7. L/SH Driver Demographic Data

Variable	Description
Age	Driver's age (years)
YrsTrucker	Number of years that the subject has been a truck driver
YrsL/SH	Number of years that the subject has been a Local/Short-Haul trucker
AvgDriveTime	Average number of minutes per day that the subject drove the truck
AvgTimeBed	Average amount of time (minutes) per night that the driver spent in bed
AvgSlpQual	Average rating of driver's self-reported sleep quality, based on a scale from 1 (terrible) to 5 (excellent)
AvgAssuSleep	Average assumed sleep time (minutes) per night calculated by the Sleepwatch program, based on the time the driver went to bed and the time he got out of bed
AvgActSleep	Average amount of actual sleep (minutes) per night as calculated by the Sleepwatch program
AvgSleepEff	Average value of sleep efficiency measure from the Sleepwatch program, derived by dividing actual sleep by time in bed and multiplying by 100

The variables AvgDriveTime, AvgTimeBed, and AvgSleepQual are based on log entries made by the drivers each day either prior to or following their work shift. AvgAssuSleep, AvgActSleep, and AvgSleepEff are derived from Actiwatch data. All values are averaged over the period of the driver's participation in the study. Because of the loss of Actiwatch data caused by a malfunction of the device, measurements of AvgAssuSleep, AvgActSleep, and AvgSleepEff are available for only 35 of the 41 drivers.

An analysis of variance was conducted to compare the mean values of the driver characteristics in Table 7 between the "High Fatigue" and "Low Fatigue" groups of drivers. ANOVA results are presented in Table 8. Boldface type indicates the driver characteristics that are significant at the 0.05 significance level. Thus, it can be seen that the driver's age and the amount of time per day he spends driving on the job are important characteristics in determining whether a driver will experience high or low levels of fatigue and drowsiness while driving. Younger drivers and those drivers who drive longer during the day are more susceptible to fatigue and drowsiness. Furthermore, drivers with more commercial driving experience tend to suffer less from the effects of drowsiness, although the relationship between years of commercial driving experience and drowsiness is only marginally significant. An interesting and somewhat surprising result from the L/SH data is that, although drivers who get more sleep appear to experience lower levels of fatigue and drowsiness, the relationship between fatigue and sleep quality/quantity is not significant. This may be attributed to the fact that overall mean values of the sleep variables, averaged over the driver's 2-week participation time in the study, are being used in the analysis.

Table 8. ANOVA Results for 41 L/SH Drivers

Dependent Variable	Mean High Fatigue	Mean Low Fatigue	F-Ratio	Pr > F
Age	26.30	35.60	11.23	0.0018
YrsTrucker	2.40	5.61	3.66	0.0632
YrsL/SH	2.29	4.83	2.28	0.1391
AvgDriveTime	207.14	162.89	4.02	0.0520
AvgTimeBed	385.45	398.19	0.69	0.4107
AvgSlpQual	3.35	3.61	2.16	0.1494
AvgAssuSleep*	341.92	371.22	2.48	0.1249
AvgActSleep*	301.79	322.57	1.49	0.2316
AvgSleepEff*	81.18	82.14	0.11	0.7478

* Determined from Actiwatch data (n = 35)

Table 8 shows the results of a one-way ANOVA test to compare population means; ANOVA is a parametric test that assumes the data come from populations with normal distributions. Another method to test for relationships between measurements is the non-parametric Spearman's rank correlation test. Spearman's rank correlation can test for relationships that are not necessarily linear. Also, it makes no assumptions about the shapes of the data distributions. The hypothesis being tested is as follows:

- H_0: There is no monotonic association between the two variables.

- H_1: There is a monotonic association between the two variables.

A monotonic association between two variables means that increases in one variable are always associated with increases in the other variable, or that increases in one variable are always associated with decreases in the other variable. Thus, Spearman's rank correlation test was used to determine whether various driver characteristics are consistently associated with a higher drowsiness index. The results are shown in Table 9. There is a significant monotonic relationship between age and drowsiness index (p-value < 0.05); that is, higher levels of fatigue are associated with younger drivers. No other variables are significantly correlated with the drowsiness index.

Table 9. Spearman's Rank Correlation of Driver Attributes with Drowsiness Index

Variable	Spearman's ρ	P-value
Age	-0.334	0.033
YrsTrucker	-0.233	0.142
YrsL/SH	-0.192	0.230
AvgDriveTime	0.251	0.114
AvgTimeBed	-0.128	0.425
AvgSlpQual	-0.137	0.395
AvgActSleep	-0.255	0.139

Logistic regression models were also developed to explore the effect of various driver demographic factors on the likelihood of a driver belonging to the "High Fatigue" group. In this analysis, odds ratios were calculated to determine the relationship of each independent variable in Table 7 to a binary dependent variable ("High Fatigue" or "Low Fatigue" driver). The logistic regression results, shown in Table 10, generally support the ANOVA results discussed previously. The 95 percent confidence intervals shown on Table 10 indicate whether the relationships between each of the driver characteristics and drowsy driving are statistically significant. The null hypothesis being tested is that the two possible outcomes, high or low driver drowsiness, are equally likely (i.e., Odds Ratio = 1). Thus, if the value of 1 is contained in the confidence interval at a 95 percent level of significance, the null hypothesis of no association cannot be rejected, and we would conclude that there is no statistical evidence in the data to suggest that drivers in a certain age group, for example, are more likely than other drivers to experience high levels of fatigue and drowsiness while driving. It must be noted that the odds ratios are based on a fairly small sample of 41 drivers.

Table 10. Logistic Regression Results for 41 L/SH Drivers

Variable	Odds Ratio	95% Confidence Interval	95% Confidence Interval
Age = 19–25 years	**8.926**	**1.262**	**100.105**
Age = 26–40 years	1.807	0.274	18.161
Age = Over 40	Reference	–	–
YrsL/SH = < 1 year	4.788	0.803	32.934
YrsL/SH = 1–5 years	0.485	0.082	2.775
YrsL/SH = > 5 years	Reference	–	–
YrsTrucker = **< 1 year**	6.926	1.141	51.683
YrsTrucker = 1–5 years	0.399	0.065	2.276
YrsTrucker = > 5 years	Reference	–	–
AvgDriveTime (= 1 if > 3 hrs, 0 otherwise)	**3.750**	**1.055**	**14.645**
AvgTimeBed (= 1 if < 6 hrs, 0 otherwise)	3.231	0.745	17.269
AvgActSleep (= 1 if < 5 hrs, 0 otherwise)	1.556	0.377	6.534
AvgSlpQual (= 1 if < 3.2, 0 otherwise)	2.618	0.708	10.610

It can be seen in Table 10 that the independent variables were separated into groups and entered into the models as categorical (i.e., 0 or 1) variables. This was done to facilitate clear and easy interpretation of the odds ratios. Age and years of commercial driving experience were both found to significantly influence whether a driver belonged to the "High Fatigue" or "Low Fatigue" group. Drivers in the 19–25-year-old age group were about nine times more likely to be "High Fatigue" drivers than older drivers. Similarly, inexperienced drivers with less than one year of CMV driving experience were approximately seven times more likely to belong to the "High Fatigue" group than more experienced drivers. The final method used to analyze the data obtained from the Task 1 video data review was a discriminant analysis to determine the feasibility of predicting whether a driver is likely to experience on-the-job fatigue and drowsiness based on such factors as age, driving experience, and sleep habits. Several discriminant functions were developed using various combinations of predictor variables from the list in Table 7, and a model that included Age, YrsL/SH, AvgDriveTime, and AvgTimeBed produced the best results.

The median Drowsiness Index for all 41 L/SH drivers is 7.35. Using this result, two groups were defined:

- Group I—High Fatigue: Fatigue Index > 7.35 ($n_1 = 20$).

- Group II—Low Fatigue: Fatigue Index ≤ 7.35 ($n_2 = 21$).

Group 1, the "High Fatigue" group consisting of 20 drivers, is defined as having a drowsiness index of greater than 7.35. Group 2, the "Low Fatigue" group consisting of 21 drivers, is defined as having a drowsiness index less than or equal to 7.35.

The following linear discriminant function was derived as shown in Figure 21:

$$D = 0.1263 \, (X_{Age} - \overline{X}_{Age}) - 0.0703 \, (X_{Yrs \, L/SH} - \overline{X}_{Yrs \, L/SH}) - 0.0078 \, (X_{AvgDriveTime} - \overline{X}_{AvgDriveTime})$$
$$+ \, 0.0078 \, (X_{AvgTimeBed} - \overline{X}_{AvgTimeBed})$$

where $\overline{X}_{Age}$ = Average age of all 41 L/SH drivers = 31.05 years
$\overline{X}_{YrsL/SH}$ = 3.59 years
$\overline{X}_{AvgDriveTime}$ = 184.47 minutes
$\overline{X}_{AvgTimeBed}$ = 391.98 minutes

Figure 21. Linear Discriminant Function

This equation shows that D is equal to 0.1263 multiplied by the difference of X subscript age and X bar subscript age, minus 0.0703 multiplied by the difference of X subscript years L/SH and X bar subscript years L/SH, minus 0.0078 multiplied by the difference of X subscript average drive time and X bar subscript average drive time, plus 0.0078 multiplied by X subscript average time in bed and X bar subscript average time in bed. X bar subscript age is equal to the average age of all 41 L/SH drivers which is equal to 31.05 years. X bar subscript years L/SH is equal to 3.59 years. X bar subscript average drive time is equal to 184.47 minutes. X bar subscript average time in bed is equal to 391.98 minutes.

The symbol D represents a discriminant score calculated from an observation not used in the estimation of the discriminant function (that is, not one of the 41 L/SH drivers). This discriminant score combines the four measurements of age, L/SH experience, daily driving time, and time in bed into a single value that may indicate whether a driver is more or less likely to experience fatigue and drowsiness while driving. As an example, consider a 30-year-old commercial driver (X_{Age} = 30) who has 5 years of local/short-haul experience ($X_{YrsL/SH}$ = 5), drives his truck an average of 4 hours per day ($X_{AvgDriveTime}$ = 240), and spends, on average, 7 hours in bed each night ($X_{AvgTimeBed}$ = 420). The discriminant function produces a score of -0.446 for this hypothetical driver. To classify this driver into either the "High Fatigue" or "Low Fatigue" group, the following decision rule is applied:

- If $D < 0$, classify the driver as belonging to Group I ("High Fatigue").
- If $D > 0$, classify the driver as belonging to Group II ("Low Fatigue").

Therefore, our hypothetical driver would be classified in the "High Fatigue" group and would be at greater risk of experiencing on-the-job drowsiness.

Once a discriminant function is established, the next step in a discriminant analysis is to evaluate the performance of the function by estimating the misclassification probability associated with the process. A matrix showing actual or observed results vs. the results predicted by the discriminant function is shown in Table 11. It can be seen that four drivers in the "High Fatigue" group are incorrectly classified as "Low Fatigue" drivers, and three drivers in the "Low Fatigue" group are misclassified.

Table 11. Discriminant Analysis Results—Actual vs. Predicted

Observed (Actual)	Classified (Predicted) I High Fatigue	Classified (Predicted) II Low Fatigue	Total
I High Fatigue	16	4	$n_1 = 20$
II Low Fatigue	3	18	$n_2 = 21$
Total	19	22	$n_1 + n_2 = 41$

Denoting the number of drivers who are misclassified as b and c for Groups I and II, respectively, the misclassification probability is shown below in Figure 22:

$$P(misclassification) = \left(\frac{b}{n_1}\right)P(I) + \left(\frac{c}{n_2}\right)P(II)$$

$$= \left(\frac{2}{20}\right)\left(\frac{20}{41}\right) + \left(\frac{3}{21}\right)\left(\frac{21}{41}\right) = \frac{7}{41} = 0.17$$

Figure 22. Misclassification Probabililty

The probability of misclassification is equal to the sum of two terms. The first term is b divided by the number of drivers in Group I times the probability of being in Group I, and the second term is c divided by the number of drivers in Group II times the probability of being in Group II. Thus, the probability of misclassification is equal to 4 divided by 20 times 20 divided by 41, plus 3 divided by 21 times 21 divided by 41, which in turn equals 7 divided by 41, or 0.17. This indicates that the discriminant function, with an error rate of 17 percent, is moderately effective in predicting highly fatigued drivers.

Table 11 indicates that 16 drivers classified or predicted to be in the "High Fatigue" group are correctly observed to be in the "High Fatigue" group, whereas four drivers classified as "Low Fatigue" drivers actually belong to the "High Fatigue" group. Furthermore, 18 drivers classified in the "Low Fatigue" group are correctly observed to be in the "Low Fatigue" group, whereas three drivers classified as "High Fatigue" drivers actually belong to the "Low Fatigue" group. Thus, the analysis predicts that 19 drivers belong to the "High Fatigue" group and 22 drivers belong to the "Low Fatigue" group, whereas the "High Fatigue" group actually consists of 20 drivers and the "Low Fatigue" group consists of 21 drivers.

3.2 FACTORS INFLUENCING DRIVER DROWSINESS: DETAILED ANALYSIS OF 1,000 EVENTS

Results from the detailed analysis of 1,000 drowsiness and baseline events are presented in this section of the report. The approach taken is to apply statistical analysis techniques to identify the driver characteristics, environmental conditions, and roadway factors that contribute to fatigue and drowsiness in L/SH truck drivers. It can be hypothesized that factors such as time of day, long work hours, poor sleep quality, monotonous driving environments, and adverse weather conditions may contribute to driver drowsiness. The analyses performed in this part of the study were designed to investigate this hypothesis. The unit of observation for these analyses is the

41

event; that is, we compared drowsiness events to a control group of baseline (ORD 1) events in order to establish relationships between drowsiness and driver/external factors.

Contingency tables were developed to determine the relationship between driver drowsiness (a drowsy vs. baseline event) and various environmental and roadway factors. The data were stratified by fatigue severity; that is, separate analyses were conducted for all events, for ORD 4 and 5 plus matching baseline events, and for ORD 2 and 3 plus matching baseline events. Complete results of the contingency table analysis are provided in appendix A. A discussion of the major findings is presented in this section.

Table 12 shows a contingency table of event category (Drowsiness vs. Baseline) as a function of time of day. A statistically significant relationship was found between drowsiness and time of day, as indicated by both the likelihood ratio chi-square statistic and the Pearson chi-square statistic (Pr > Chi-Square = 0.044). Comparing row percentages for baseline and drowsiness events on Table 12, a higher propensity for drowsiness is observed during the period of 6 a.m. to 9 a.m. (i.e., 32.5 percent of all fatigue events occur during this time period, as compared to only 24.3 percent of baseline events) and a lower tendency for drowsiness is seen in the time period from 9 a.m. to 3 p.m.

Table 12. Contingency Table of Event Category by Time of Day

Event Category	3–6 a.m.	6–9 a.m.	9 a.m.–12 p.m.	12–3 p.m.	3–6 p.m.	6–9 p.m.	Total
Baseline Count	20	91	63	98	90	13	–
Baseline Col %	33.9	32.27	47.37	42.79	39.65	39.39	–
Baseline Row %	5.33	24.27	16.80	26.13	24.00	3.47	375
Fatigue Count	39	191	70	131	137	20	–
Fatigue Col %	66.10	67.73	52.63	57.21	60.35	60.61	–
Fatigue Row %	6.63	32.48	11.90	22.28	23.30	3.40	588
Total	59	282	133	229	227	33	963

The relationship between event category and traffic density is shown in Table 13. There turned out to be a significant association between traffic density and driver drowsiness (Pr > Chi-Square = 0.015); however, the relationship was surprising and counterintuitive. It is seen on Table 13 that 26 out of the 31 events that were recorded when traffic volume was moderately heavy (i.e., Level of Service [LOS] C, D, or E), or about 84 percent, involved driver drowsiness. This is in contrast to 60 percent of the events in light traffic involving drowsiness. Thus, while driving in heavier traffic might be expected to keep a driver alert and focused, our results seem to suggest that drivers are more likely to experience drowsiness in heavier traffic. A possible explanation for this unexpected result is bias caused by the low number of observations in heavy traffic; most of the driving in the L/SH field study took place on rural roads with low traffic volume. This explanation is validated to some degree when LOS B, C, D, and E events are combined and compared to free-flow traffic conditions (LOS A). In this case, 61.9 percent of LOS B/C/D/E events involve fatigue as compared to 60.3 percent of LOS A events, and this difference is not statistically significant.

Table 13. Contingency Table of Event Category by Traffic Density

Event Category	LOS A	LOS B	LOS C/D/E	Total
Baseline Count	**305**	**83**	**5**	
Baseline Col %	39.66	41.50	16.13	
Baseline Row %	77.61	21.12	1.27	**393**
Fatigue Count	**464**	**117**	**26**	
Fatigue Col %	60.34	58.50	83.87	
Fatigue Row %	76.44	19.28	4.38	**607**
Total	**769**	**200**	**31**	**1000**

Table 14 is a contingency table of weather conditions by event category. Examining the column percentages, we see that 62.2 percent of the events occurring in clear weather and 60.8 percent of those occurring in cloudy conditions are drowsy events; however, of the events observed when it was raining or snowing, only 51.8 percent were drowsy events. Therefore, drowsiness appears to be less likely to occur in poor weather conditions, but this relationship between drowsiness and weather conditions was not statistically significant (Pr > Chi-Square = 0.117).

Table 14. Contingency Table of Event Category by Weather Conditions

Event Category	Clear	Cloudy	Rain/Snow	Total
Baseline Count	**246**	**93**	**54**	
Baseline Col %	37.79	39.24	48.21	
Baseline Row %	62.60	23.66	13.74	**393**
Fatigue Count	**405**	**144**	**58**	
Fatigue Col %	62.21	60.76	51.79	
Fatigue Row %	66.72	23.72	9.56	**607**
Total	**651**	**237**	**112**	**1000**

Looking at the effect of road surface condition on drowsy driving in Table 15, it can be seen that 61.5 percent of all the events observed on dry roads involved driver drowsiness, whereas only 53.4 percent of the events occurring on wet pavement were drowsy events. This indicates that drowsiness is somewhat less prevalent when roads are wet; however, both the likelihood ratio and Pearson chi-square statistics show that the relationship is not statistically significant (Pr > Chi-Square = 0.11).

Table 15. Contingency Table of Event Category by Road Surface Condition

Event Category	Dry	Wet	Total
Baseline Count	**345**	**48**	
Baseline Col %	38.46	46.60	
Baseline Row %	87.79	12.21	**393**
Fatigue Count	**552**	**55**	
Fatigue Col %	61.54	53.40	
Fatigue Row %	90.94	9.06	**607**
Total	**897**	**103**	**1000**

Table 16 shows the relationship between event category and visibility conditions. Similar to the breakdown by weather conditions as shown in Table 14, drowsiness was observed in a smaller proportion of events that occurred in rain, snow, or fog (51 percent) than in any other visibility conditions (61 percent in unlimited visibility, 70 percent in dark/twilight, and 66 percent in sun/glare). But once again, there was no statistically significant association between drowsiness and visibility ($Pr > Chi\text{-}Square = 0.098$). Weather conditions, road conditions, and visibility conditions are all clearly related; when it is raining, for example, the roads are wet and visibility is reduced. So, as expected, the analysis of the relationship between these environmental factors and drowsy driving produced similar and consistent results.

Table 16. Contingency Table of Event by Visibility Conditions

Event Category	Unlimited	Rain/Snow/Fog	Dark/Twilight	Sun Glare	Total
Baseline Count	**310**	**46**	**15**	**22**	
Baseline Col %	39.19	48.94	30.00	33.85	
Baseline Row %	78.88	11.70	3.82	5.60	**393**
Fatigue Count	**481**	**48**	**35**	**43**	
Fatigue Col %	60.81	51.06	70.00	66.15	
Fatigue Row %	79.24	7.91	5.77	7.08	**607**
Total	**651**	**237**	**112**		**1000**

 The results of the contingency table analysis of event category by outside light condition are shown in Table 17. The incidence of drowsiness while driving is significantly associated with light condition ($Pr > Chi\text{-}Square = 0.047$). A comparison of column percentages in Table 17 suggests that drowsiness is relatively less prevalent during daylight hours (57.8 percent of events) than at dawn (65.7 percent) or dusk/night (64.5 percent). It should be noted that this is consistent with the positive association seen previously between drowsiness and time of day.

**Table 17. Contingency Table of Event Category
by Outside Light Condition**

Event Category	Dawn	Daylight	Dusk/Night	Total
Baseline Count	**118**	**264**	**11**	
Baseline Col %	34.30	42.24	35.48	
Baseline Row %	30.03	67.18	2.80	**393**
Fatigue Count	**226**	**361**	**20**	
Fatigue Col %	65.70	57.76	64.52	
Fatigue Row %	37.23	59.47	3.29	**607**
Total	**344**	**625**	**31**	**1000**

The contingency table analysis results presented up to this point have been based on all 1,000 drowsy and baseline events. Separate analyses were also conducted using only the most severe drowsy episodes, those with an ORD rating of 4 or 5, and their matching baseline events. For the more severe drowsy events, another factor, road geometry, proved to be positively associated with drowsiness. Table 18 is a contingency table of event category by road geometry for ORD 4 and 5 and matching baseline events. Looking at the column percentages, we can see that the proportion of events occurring on straight and curved roadways is fairly evenly split between drowsy and baseline events; that is, approximately 49 percent of events on straight or curved roads involve drowsiness, whereas 51 percent do not involve drowsiness. The results, however, are quite different at intersections and "other" road configurations, where 87 percent of the recorded events involve driver drowsiness. This is a surprising result, since drivers would be expected to be more alert and attentive at intersections as opposed to straight, open highways. It is hypothesized that this is most likely attributable to selection bias, rather than reflecting a real effect of roadway configuration. The majority of matching baseline events that were selected for each ORD 4 and ORD 5 event at an intersection also did not take place at an intersection, but instead occurred on the highway away from a junction or intersection.

Table 18. Contingency Table of Event Category by Road Geometry

Event Category	Straightaway	Curve	Intersection	Other	Total
Baseline Count	**182**	**99**	**1**	**3**	
Baseline Col %	51.41	51.30	9.09	25.00	
Baseline Row %	63.86	34.74	0.35	1.05	**285**
Fatigue Count	**172**	**94**	**10**	**9**	
Fatigue Col %	48.59	48.70	90.91	75.00	
Fatigue Row %	60.35	32.98	3.51	3.16	**285**
Total	**354**	**193**	**11**	**12**	**570**

The relationship between ORD 4 and ORD 5 drowsy events and time of day is shown in Table 19. As shown previously in Table 12 for all events, drowsiness is more prevalent and occurs more frequently in the time period of 6 a.m. to 9 a.m. than in any other period during the day.

Approximately 64 percent of all events occurring between 6 a.m. and 9 a.m. are fatigue events, a higher percentage than at any other time of day. Also, looking at row percentages, it can be seen that more than one-third of all drowsy events occur between the hours of 6 a.m. and 9 a.m.

Table 19. Contingency Table of Event Category by Time of Day for ORD 4 & ORD 5 Events

Event Category	3–6 a.m.	6–9 a.m.	9 a.m.–12 p.m.	12–3 p.m.	3–6 p.m.	6–9 p.m.	Total
Baseline Count	**14**	**57**	**45**	**81**	**65**	**10**	–
Baseline Col %	445.16	36.31	61.64	55.86	51.59	76.92	–
Baseline Row %	5.15	20.96	16.54	29.78	23.90	3.68	**272**
Fatigue Count	**17**	**100**	**28**	**64**	**61**	**3**	–
Fatigue Col %	54.84	63.69	38.36	44.14	48.41	23.08	–
Fatigue Row %	6.23	36.63	10.26	23.44	22.34	1.10	**273**
Total	**31**	**157**	**73**	**145**	**126**	**13**	**545**

A strong positive association between fatigue and time of day was clearly established in this analysis. It is interesting and informative to examine more closely the specific hours of the workday that are most problematic for these L/SH drivers. Because every occurrence of a severe ORD 4 and 5 episode of drowsiness was analyzed in detail during the Task 2 video reduction/archiving process, an accurate picture of when these episodes take place is obtained, as a function of both time of day and time since the driver's shift began (i.e., time on duty). The distribution of ORD 4 and 5 events by time of day and time on duty are displayed in Figure 23 and Figure 24, respectively.

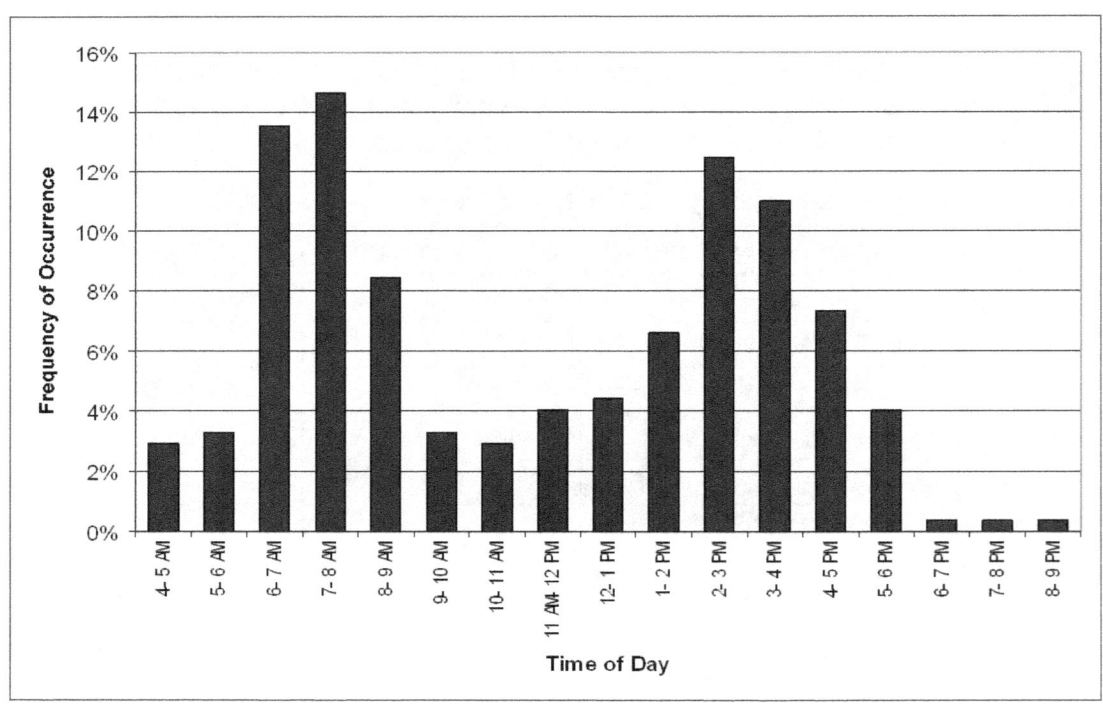

Figure 23. Frequency Distribution of ORD 4 and 5 Events by Time of Day

46

Figure 23 is a histogram showing the frequency of occurrence on the y-axis as a function of time of day in one-hour increments on the x-axis. Figure 23 shows that the highest incident rate of drowsiness (approximately 15 percent of all ORD 4 and 5 events) occurs between 7 and 8 a.m., followed by the 6–7 a.m. time period at nearly 14 percent. As late morning and early afternoon approach, the rate decreases significantly to 4 percent or less, but then rises again between 2 and 4 p.m. to about 12 percent. Finally, the frequency of occurrence drops off to less than 1 percent between 6 and 9 p.m. The high incidence early in the morning most likely reflects the drivers' difficulty in waking up, and it was during this time period that we observed frequent yawning and heavy eyes. The increase in afternoon drowsy occurrences may be caused by a loss of energy due to fatigue, sleep deprivation, or each individual driver's circadian rhythm.

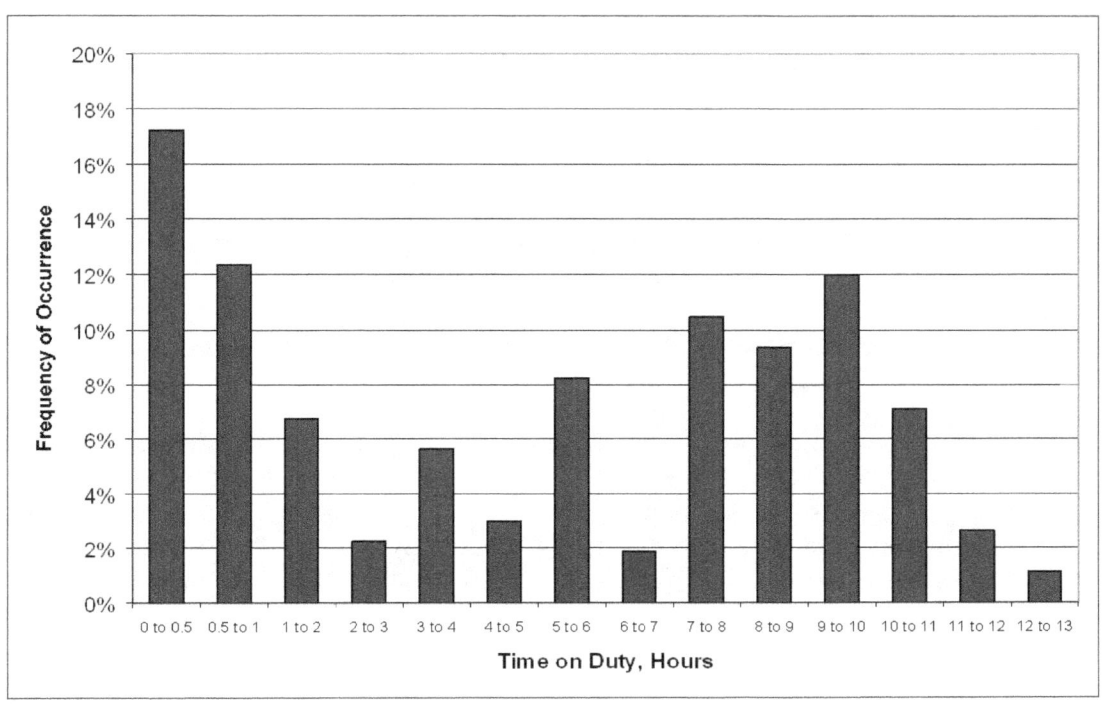

Figure 24. Frequency Distribution of ORD 4 and 5 Events by Time of Day

Although L/SH drivers begin and end their workdays at their home base and sleep at home every night, there are driver-to-driver differences as to when the work shift begins, as well as day-to-day differences for individual drivers. Hence, the distribution by time on duty in Figure 24 looks somewhat different than the frequency distribution by time of day shown in Figure 23. Figure 24 is a histogram showing the frequency of occurrence on the y-axis as a function of time on duty in 1-hour increments on the x-axis (note that the first two bars represent half-hour increments). Consistent with the notion that some drivers may not be "morning people," the highest rate of ORD 4 and 5 drowsy episodes (more than 17 percent) occurs in the initial half-hour of the drivers' work shift, and about 30 percent of all severe drowsy events occur within the first hour. The results in Figure 24 also suggest that drowsiness becomes a problem when the driver has been on duty for 7 to 10 hours; the frequencies of occurrence in these time periods are between 9 and 12 percent. The lowest frequencies of occurrence are 1 to 2 percent, and they are found when the drivers have been on duty for 2–3 hours, 6–7 hours, and 12–13 hours.

The relationships between drowsy driving and both sleep quantity and time on duty were investigated using Analysis of Variance. Two measures of sleep quantity were evaluated: the amount of actual sleep measured by Actiwatch data and the amount of time spent in bed reported by the drivers in a daily sleep log. Time in bed is a proxy for actual sleep duration; however, researchers at the Walter Reed Army Institute of Research stated in their study of the effects of sleep schedules on CMV driver performance that time spent in bed is not a good predictor of sleep duration (Balkin et al., 2000). Time in bed was used in the current study because data was available for all 41 drivers, whereas usable Actiwatch data were obtained for only 35 drivers due to technical problems with the Actiwatch wrist monitor. The Walter Reed project (Balkin et al., 2000) included a sleep dose/response laboratory study that focused on quantifying the relationship between nighttime sleep duration and subsequent performance across 7 consecutive days. It was found that a reduction in average nighttime sleep duration resulted in a measurable performance degradation among CMV drivers and that this decrement in performance was maintained across 7 consecutive days of sleep restriction. It was also found that following severe sleep restriction (a total of 3 hours of sleep per night), recovery of performance was not complete even after 3 consecutive nights of recovery sleep (8 hours spent in bed each night). The researchers concluded that the existing level of daytime alertness and performance capacity is a function not only of an individual's circadian rhythm, time since the last sleep period, and duration of the last sleep period, but also of sleep history extending back for at least several days. Thus, on the basis of this important information, the relationship between drowsy events and sleep duration (i.e., actual sleep and time in bed) one, two, and three nights prior to the event was investigated.

ANOVA results using all 1,000 drowsy and baseline events indicated no statistically significant association between drowsiness and time in bed. The researchers found that the previous night's actual sleep duration was associated with the occurrence of drowsiness. The average actual sleep duration the night before a drowsy event was 285 minutes, as compared to 298 minutes for baseline events (p-value = 0.018). No association was found between drowsiness and sleep duration 2 and 3 nights prior to drowsy events. In addition, a statistically significant difference in the mean values of time on duty was found between drowsiness and baseline events (Mean Drowsiness = 320 minutes; Mean Baseline = 362 minutes; p-value = 0.0094). Interestingly, no significant relationships were found between any measures of sleep duration and drowsiness when only the more severe ORD 4 and ORD 5 events were analyzed. There was, however, a significant association between drowsiness and time on duty (Mean Drowsiness = 307 minutes; Mean Baseline = 377 minutes; p-value = 0.0005). These results indicate that, on average, drivers are more alert later in the work day, and this is consistent with the earlier findings that drowsiness seems to be a problem for these drivers early in their shifts, between 6 a.m. and 9 a.m. Finally, no significant differences in sleep quantity or time of day were found between ORD 2 and 3 events and baseline events.

The primary quantitative measure of drowsiness determined during the detailed video data analysis was PERCLOS, the proportion of time over the 3-minute interval that the driver's eyes were closed or nearly closed. An analysis using stepwise linear regression was conducted to identify the factors that have a significant impact on PERCLOS. Separate regression models were estimated for: 1) the entire data set (i.e., all 1,000 events), 2) ORD 4 and ORD 5 fatigue events plus matching baseline events, and 3) ORD 2 and ORD 3 events plus matching baseline events. Table 20, Table 21 and Table 22 show the output of the regression analysis for these three models, including the parameter estimate, the t-ratio, and p-value for each variable. It should be noted that the default for a variable being removed from the model is $p > 0.05$.

Table 20. Regression Model to Identify Factors Affecting PERCLOS (All Events; R2 = 0.077)

Variable	Parameter Estimate	t-Ratio	Prob > | t |
Intercept	-0.7982	-1.53	0.1253
TIME1	2.7901	4.35	<0.0001
TIME2	2.2750	5.92	<0.0001
TIME5	0.8121	2.43	0.0153
POORSLEEP	2.2160	4.29	<0.0001
FAIRSLEEP	1.0364	2.57	0.0103
DENSITY	-0.8022	-2.61	0.0093
MIDLANE	1.3142	2.44	0.0151
URBANDIV	0.7455	2.22	0.0268
BADVISION	-0.7653	-2.41	0.0163
DAYLIGHT	0.8874	2.32	0.0203

Table 21. Regression Model to Identify Factors Affecting PERCLOS (ORD 4 & 5 Events; R2 = 0.089).

Variable	Parameter Estimate	t-Ratio	Prob > | t |
Intercept	2.8347	7.41	<0.0001
TIME2	2.0176	3.87	0.0001
TIME4	-1.2574	-2.38	0.0177
POORSLEEP	1.3413	2.34	0.0195
DENSITY	-1.4528	-2.74	0.0063
RURALUNDIV	-1.3920	-2.67	0.0078
URBANUNDIV	-1.8782	-2.16	0.0309

Table 22. Regression Model to Identify Factors Affecting PERCLOS (ORD 2 & 3 Events; R2 = 0.090)

Variable	Parameter Estimate	t-Ratio	Prob > | t |
Intercept	0.7586	8.29	<0.0001
YrsTrucker	-0.0498	-3.24	0.0013
TIME1	1.6808	6.25	<0.0001

The variables in the models are indicator or "dummy" variables that have a value of 0 or 1. They are defined as follows:

- TIME1 = 1 if Time of Day is between 3 a.m. and 6 a.m.; = 0 otherwise.

- TIME2 = 1 if Time of Day is between 6 a.m. and 9 a.m.; = 0 otherwise.

- TIME4 = 1 if Time of Day is between 12 p.m. and 3 p.m.; = 0 otherwise.

- TIME5 = 1 if Time of Day is between 3 p.m. and 6 p.m.; = 0 otherwise.

- POORSLEEP = 1 if driver's self-reported assessment of his previous night's sleep quality is Poor (SlpQual = 1 or 2); = 0 otherwise.

- FAIRSLEEP = 1 if driver's self-reported assessment of his previous night's sleep quality is Fair (SlpQual = 3 or 4); = 0 otherwise.

- DENSITY = 1 if traffic volume is LOS B, C, D, or E; = 0 otherwise.

- MIDLANE = 1 if the driver is driving in the middle lane of a multi-lane highway at the time of the event; = 0 otherwise.

- URBANDIV = 1 if the driver is driving on a divided highway in an urban area at the time of the event; = 0 otherwise.

- URBANUNDIV = 1 if the driver is driving on an undivided road in an urban area at the time of the event; = 0 otherwise.

- RURALUNDIV = 1 if the driver is driving on an undivided road in a rural area at the time of the event; = 0 otherwise.

- BADVISION = 1 if outside visibility conditions are poor (i.e., rain, snow, fog, darkness, or sun glare); = 0 otherwise

- DAYLIGHT = 1 if the event takes place during daylight; = 0 otherwise.

- YrsTrucker (not an indicator variable) = the driver's number of years of commercial driving experience.

When analyzing all 1,000 events (Table 20), the stepwise regression results indicate that the following factors were statistically significantly associated with an increase in PERCLOS (that is, an increased level of fatigue or drowsiness):

- Time of day between 3 a.m. and 9 a.m. and between 3 p.m. and 6 p.m.

- Poor and fair sleep quality.

- Traveling in the middle lane of a multilane highway.

- Traveling on a divided highway in an urban area.

- Driving during daylight hours (as opposed to dawn, dusk, or nighttime).

Also, Table 13 shows that traffic density (heavier traffic volume) and poor visibility are related to a decrease in PERCLOS.

It is important to keep in mind that the purpose of the linear regression analysis is to identify possible driver and environmental variables that may contribute to on-the-job fatigue; the regression models do not imply or determine causality. Thus, we are not suggesting that driving in the middle lane, for example, causes fatigue or drowsiness. Rather, the interpretation of the parameter estimate of 1.3142 for the variable MIDLANE is that an increase in PERCLOS of about 1.3 percent was observed when drivers were traveling in the middle lane of a multi-lane highway. In a similar manner, these results show that an increase in PERCLOS of 2.3 percent was observed for all events occurring between 6 a.m. and 9 a.m. and that a 2.2 percent increase in PERCLOS can be expected when a driver's self-assessment of his previous night's sleep quality is rated as poor. Conversely, a decrease in PERCLOS (i.e., improved alertness and less drowsiness) of approximately 0.8 percent was observed in poor visibility conditions. Intuitively, this is a reasonable outcome, since environmental conditions such as rain, fog, or sun glare may tend to break the monotony and boredom of driving.

For the more severe drowsy events (ORD 4 and 5) shown in Table 21, a higher PERCLOS value was associated with poor sleep quality and time of day between 6 a.m. and 9 a.m. Here again, the drivers seem to have difficulty waking up and exhibit signs of drowsiness (heavy eyelids and eye closings) early in the morning. On the other hand, more alert and awake driving was observed between noon and 3 p.m., as well as in heavier traffic conditions and on undivided roadways, in both rural and urban areas. The result that a lower incidence of drowsiness is associated with driving in heavier traffic and on roadways with no physical barriers separating traffic in opposite-direction travel lanes is not unexpected, since these conditions present the driver with a more challenging driving environment.

Table 22 indicates that years of commercial driving experience and the period of time from 3 a.m. to 6 a.m. are the only variables significantly related to changes in PERCLOS for mild and moderate drowsy episodes. Furthermore, it should be pointed out that although the effect of driving experience on PERCLOS is statistically significant, the small coefficient on the variable "YrsTrucker" implies that it is of little practical significance. In other words, determining that, all else being equal, PERCLOS can be expected to decrease by 0.05 percent for each additional year of commercial driving experience does not suggest a significant safety benefit among more experienced drivers.

The final analytical approach applied to the detailed data reduction of 1,000 events was logistic regression. Odds ratios were computed for each variable or risk factor to determine which factors increase the likelihood of drowsy driving. The binary dependent variable used in the logistic regression models was the occurrence of fatigue/drowsiness (Yes or No). The odds ratio for each risk factor was adjusted for the potential confounding effect of age, since the earlier analysis of all fatigue events revealed a significant relationship between a driver's age and fatigue. Odds ratios for fatigue events compared to baseline events are presented in Table 23 for all events, severe (ORD 4 and 5) fatigue and matched baseline events, and mild/moderate (ORD 2 and 3) fatigue and matched baseline events. Ninety-five percent confidence intervals are shown in parentheses; a confidence interval containing the value 1 for a particular risk factor indicates the lack of a statistically significant relationship (or no increase in the likelihood of fatigue) between that factor and drowsy driving. Significant relationships are highlighted in boldface type in Table 23.

The logistic regression results presented in Table 23 show that sleep quantity and quality, traffic density, road geometry, road surface condition, and visibility conditions had no impact on the likelihood of the occurrence of fatigue. Consistent with previous analyses, we see that drowsiness was about twice as likely to occur between 6 a.m. and 9 a.m. as compared to baseline. And we can also see that severe episodes of drowsiness are nearly three times as likely to occur between 6 a.m. and 9 a.m. as compared to baseline. Driving in the right lane of a multi-lane highway was found to increase the likelihood of drowsiness by about 36 percent, whereas driving during daylight hours (as opposed to at dawn, dusk, or nighttime) and driving in rainy weather both *decreased* the likelihood of fatigue. Mild and moderate fatigue events (ORD 2 and 3) were only about half as likely to occur on undivided roadways in urban areas as compared to baseline. Considering only the most severe drowsy events (ORD 4 and 5), episodes of drowsiness and fatigue were only half as likely to occur when the driver had been on duty for 4 to 6 hours after the beginning of the work shift. Moreover, mild and moderate episodes of drowsiness were found to be nearly three times more likely to occur near the end of the work shift when the driver had been on duty between 6 and 8 hours. Therefore, our analysis provides fairly strong evidence that fatigue and drowsiness were problematic for these L/SH drivers early in the morning as they began their workday and again, to a lesser extent, near the end of the work shift

Table 23. Calculated Odds Ratios for Fatigue vs. Baseline Events

Risk Factor	Adjusted Odds Ratio (95% C.I.) All Events	Adjusted Odds Ratio (95% C.I.) ORD 4 & 5 Events	Adjusted Odds Ratio (95% C.I.) ORD 2 & 3 Events
Time of Day:	–	–	–
3 a.m.–6 a.m.	1.659 (0.881–3.190)	1.897 (0.808–4.523)	1.575 (0.567–4.860)
6 a.m.–9 a.m.	**1.943 (1.271–2.972)**	**2.818 (1.598–5.043)**	1.142 (0.569–2.249)
9 a.m.–12 p.m.	Ref.	Ref.	Ref.
12 p.m.–3 p.m.	1.189 (0.773–1.829)	1.260 (0.711–2.254)	1.666 (0.772–3.616)
3 p.m.–6 p.m.	1.359 (0.881–2.096)	1.490 (0.830–2.702)	1.301 (0.632–2.651)
6 p.m.–9 p.m.	1.184 (0.541–2.662)	0.449 (0.093–1.659)	2.447 (0.701–11.497)
Previous Night's Sleep Quality:	–	–	–
Poor	0.838 (0.482–1.452)	1.530 (0.662–3.617)	1.052 (0.409–2.880)
Fair	1.019 (0.658–1.560)	1.521 (0.730–3.260)	1.283 (0.701–2.284)
Good/Excellent	Ref.	Ref.	Ref.
Time on Duty:	–	–	–
0–2 Hours	1.553 (0.887–2.694)	1.215 (0.572–2.532)	2.080 (0.888–4.780)
2–4 Hours	Ref.	Ref.	Ref.
4–6 Hours	0.755 (0.409–1.383)	**0.428 (0.189–0.948)**	2.320 (0.838–6.594)
6–8 Hours	1.113 (0.606–2.031)	0.574 (0.253–1.278)	**2.881 (1.091–7.728)**
> 8 Hours	0.947 (0.547–1.622)	0.585 (0.280–1.198)	2.174 (0.924–5.022)

Risk Factor	Adjusted Odds Ratio (95% C.I.) All Events	Adjusted Odds Ratio (95% C.I.) ORD 4 & 5 Events	Adjusted Odds Ratio (95% C.I.) ORD 2 & 3 Events
Time in Bed Previous Night:	–	–	–
< 5 Hours	1.616 (0.660–3.927)	3.006 (0.862–12.314)	0.712 (0.099–3.296)
5–6 Hours	1.356 (0.592–3.066)	2.411 (0.762–9.158)	0.639 (0.093–2.675)
6–7 Hours	1.132 (0.495–2.554)	2.683 (0.861–10.084)	0.453 (0.066–1.904)
7–8 Hours	1.311 (0.573–2.956)	2.457 (0.783–9.275)	0.669 (0.098–2.802)
> 8 Hours	Ref.	Ref.	Ref.
Traffic Density:	–	–	–
LOS A	Ref.	Ref.	Ref.
LOS B/C/D/E	1.078 (0.797–1.462)	0.919 (0.613–1.375)	1.129 (0.685–1.904)
Lane Position:	–	–	–
N/A	Ref.	Ref.	Ref.
Right	**1.365 (1.008–1.848)**	1.027 (0.692–1.527)	1.609 (0.948–2.706)
Middle	1.668 (0.919–3.129)	1.903 (0.871–4.322)	1.443 (0.549–4.279)
Left	0.923 (0.621–1.374)	0.856 (0.521–1.403)	1.018 (0.503–2.103)
Ramp	1.939 (0.923–4.374)	1.753 (0.740–4.372)	4.555 (0.818–8.542)
Type of Roadway:	–	–	–
Rural Divided	Ref.	Ref.	Ref.
Rural Undivided	0.763 (0.538–1.084)	0.952 (0.621–1.458)	1.033 (0.500–2.310)
Urban Divided	0.997 (0.714–1.400)	1.360 (0.885–2.097)	0.738 (0.421–1.325)
Urban Undivided	0.735 (0.453–1.198)	1.060 (0.543–2.068)	**0.464 (0.225–0.980)**
Road Geometry:	–	–	–
Straight	1.072 (0.809–1.417)	0.853 (0.603–1.207)	1.389 (0.830–2.303)
Curved/Intersection	Ref.	Ref.	Ref.
Road Surface Condition:	–	–	–
Dry	Ref.	Ref.	Ref.
Wet	0.737 (0.488–1.115)	0.875 (0.523–1.458)	0.614 (0.299–1.320)
Weather:	–	–	–

Risk Factor	Adjusted Odds Ratio (95% C.I.) All Events	Adjusted Odds Ratio (95% C.I.) ORD 4 & 5 Events	Adjusted Odds Ratio (95% C.I.) ORD 2 & 3 Events
Clear/Dry	Ref.	Ref.	Ref.
Cloudy	0.936 (0.690–1.273)	0.835 (0.553–1.259)	0.929 (0.566–1.551)
Rain	**0.668** **(0.446–1.003)**	0.824 (0.501–1.379)	0.523 (0.252–1.121)
Visibility:	–	–	–
Unlimited	Ref.	Ref.	Ref.
Rain/Fog/Dark/Glare	0.972 (0.713–1.332)	0.838 (0.537v1.303)	0.812 (0.504–1.328)
Lighting Conditions:	–	–	–
Daylight	**0.723** **(0.553–0.942)**	**0.653** **(0.460–0.926)**	1.015 (0.651v1.574)
Dawn/Dusk/Night	Ref.	Ref.	Ref.

3.3 RELATIONSHIP OF DRIVER FATIGUE AND DRIVER PERFORMANCE

The objective of this task was to compare the driving performance of L/SH truck operators during periods of drowsiness with their driving performance during baseline periods of normal, alert driving to determine if drowsiness impacts driving performance. It might be expected that drivers having trouble staying awake will experience difficulty in maintaining their vehicles' velocity and lane position. Hence, two measures of driver performance, lane-keeping and speed management, were evaluated in an effort to correlate driver drowsiness and performance.

The vehicle engineering and performance data collected during the L/SH field study included measurements of velocity and steering position; however, the onboard instrumentation hardware did not include lane-tracking sensors for measuring lane position. Due to the amount of "play" in the steering columns of the trucks used on the L/SH field study, variations in steering position did not accurately translate to variations in lane position. Therefore, investigation of a driver's lane-keeping performance was limited to observational analysis of video data. Severe degradation of lane-keeping ability and obvious lane excursions were apparent in the video data, but variations in vehicle position within the lane and minor lane drifting were not easily detectable.

In this study, an event having an ORD value of 5 is defined as one that has an impact on driving ability or performance. The overwhelming majority of ORD 5 events involved lane violations (one instance of a drowsy driver involved in a rear-end near-collision was observed). Thus, the frequency and rate of occurrence of ORD 5 events can give a rough idea of the extent to which fatigue and drowsiness affect a driver's ability to maintain lane position. A total of 125 ORD 5 events were observed, or 4.5 percent of the total number of drowsy events identified in this study. For all drivers collectively, the rate of occurrence of ORD 5 events is about one event for every 7 hours of driving. Nineteen of the 41 drivers who participated in the L/SH study showed signs of impaired driving performance due to fatigue, and two drivers were found to be particularly serious offenders. These two drivers experienced drowsy episodes that resulted in degraded driving performance at the rate of one episode for every 54 and 63 minutes of driving, respectively.

A random sample of 50 ORD 4 and 5 events was chosen to explore the effect of drowsiness on a driver's ability to control vehicle speed. The criterion for selecting these 3-minute events was that the actual duration of the drowsy episode be between 1 and 2 minutes. The idea behind this approach was to select a single 3-minute segment of driving in which the driver started out awake and alert before lapsing into drowsiness. The vehicle velocity data were matched to the corresponding video segment by sync number, and the data were then studied to compare velocity variations before and after the onset of fatigue. An attempt was made to detect evidence of "lead foot syndrome," or significant variability in vehicle speed, when the driver became drowsy.

Examples of the results of this analysis are shown in Figure 25–Figure 32. Each figure shows individual measurements of velocity as a function of time, as well as a graph of the moving range of the velocity over the 3-minute event segment length. The moving range of two successive observations, defined as $MR_i = |X_i - X_{i-1}|$, can be used as a quick visual means to estimate variability in the data. (The equation reads MR subscript i is equal to the absolute value of the difference of X subscript i minus X subscript i-1.). For clarity, the data were filtered to show one data point per second rather than 10 data points per second (as they are recorded by the onboard data acquisition system). Note that the point in time at which the driver became drowsy is indicated on each individual measurement chart.

Figure 25 shows velocity in miles per hour on the y-axis as a function of time on the x-axis. The time scale is from 0 to 180 seconds. The velocity is a fairly smooth curve beginning and ending at just below 70 mi/h. The average velocity for the 3-minute interval is 69.93 mi/h. At approximately 80 seconds, the velocity drops to about 60 mi/h, and at 145 seconds the velocity increases to about 76 mi/h for a duration of about 10 seconds. There is a notation on the chart that the onset of fatigue occurs at 97.8 seconds.

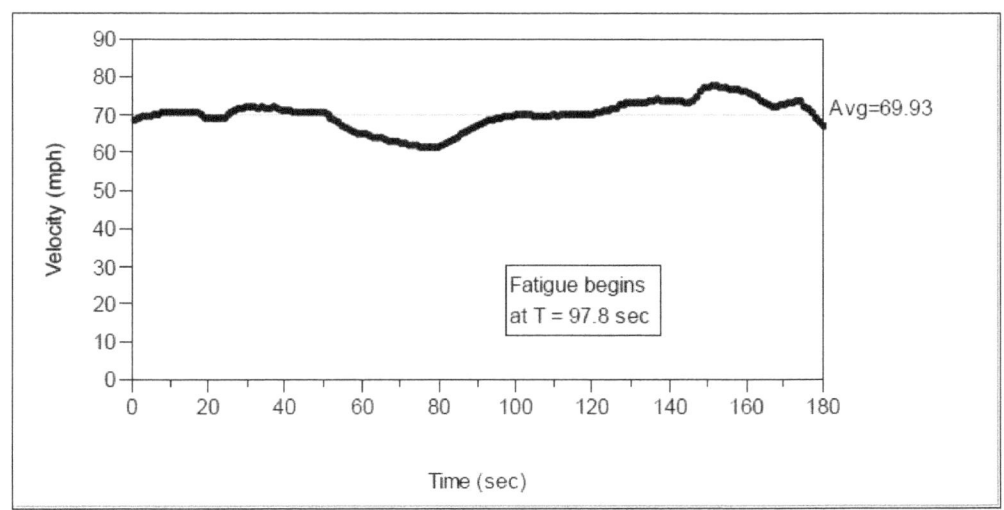

Figure 25. Individual Measurement of Velocity vs. Time (Subject 12, Event #50)

The moving range of velocity in miles per hour is shown on the vertical axis of Figure 26 as a function of time over a 180-second interval. The average value of the moving range is 0.289 mi/h. Prior to the onset of fatigue at 97.8 seconds, there are six values of moving range at approximately 0.85 mi/h and numerous values just below 0.6 mi/h. After 97.8 seconds, there are five values at 1.1 mi/h and two values at 1.4 mi/h. Both before and after fatigue onset at 97.8 seconds, there are numerous moving range points at 0.

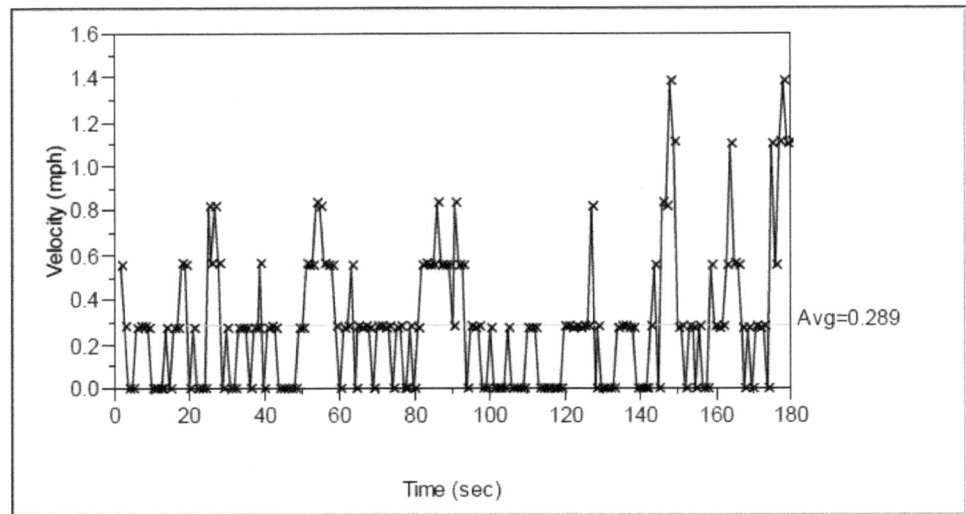

Figure 26. Moving Range of Velocity vs. Time (Subject 12, Event #50)

Figure 27 shows velocity in miles per hour on the y-axis as a function of time on the x-axis. The time scale is from 0 to 180 seconds. The velocity is a fairly smooth curve beginning and ending at just below 60 mi/h. The average velocity for the 3-minute interval is 56.43 mi/h, and it ranges between approximately 52 and 62 mi/h. There is a notation on the chart that the onset of fatigue begins at 88.9 seconds.

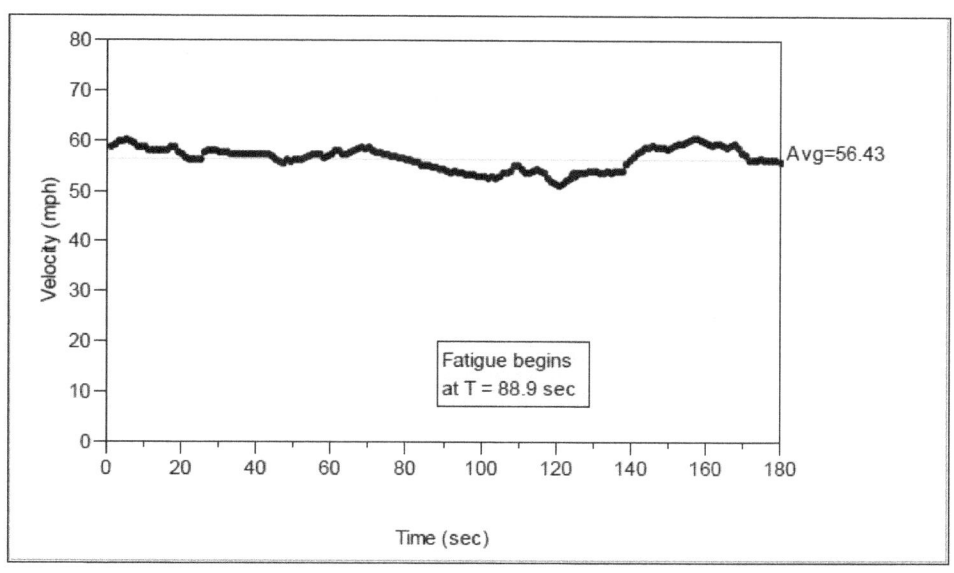

Figure 27. Individual Measurement of Velocity vs. Time (Subject 15, Event #38)

The moving range of velocity in miles per hour is shown on the vertical axis in Figure 28 as a function of time over a 180-second interval. The average value of the moving range is 0.302 mi/h. Prior to the onset of fatigue at 88.9 seconds, there is one value of moving range at 1.4 mi/h and three values at approximately 0.85 mi/h, and numerous values just below 0.6 mi/h. After 88.9 seconds, there is one value at 1.4 mi/h, one value at 1.1 mi/h, and eight values at 0.85 mi/h. Thus, there appears to be greater speed variability after the onset of fatigue. Both before and after fatigue onset at 88.9 seconds, there are numerous moving range points at 0.3 and at 0.

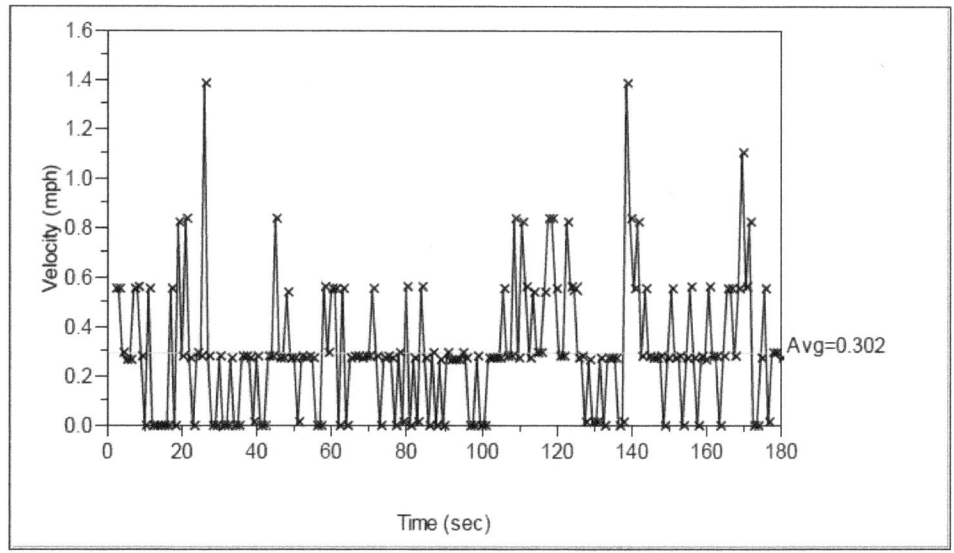

Figure 28. Moving Range of Velocity vs. Time (Subject 15, Event #38)

Figure 29 shows velocity in miles per hour on the y-axis as a function of time on the x-axis. The time scale is from 0 to 180 seconds. The velocity curve oscillates slightly in a sinusoidal fashion within a narrow range of 60 and 66 mi/h. Velocity begins and ends at the overall 3-minute average value of 64 mi/h. There is a notation on the chart that the onset of fatigue begins at 74.2 seconds.

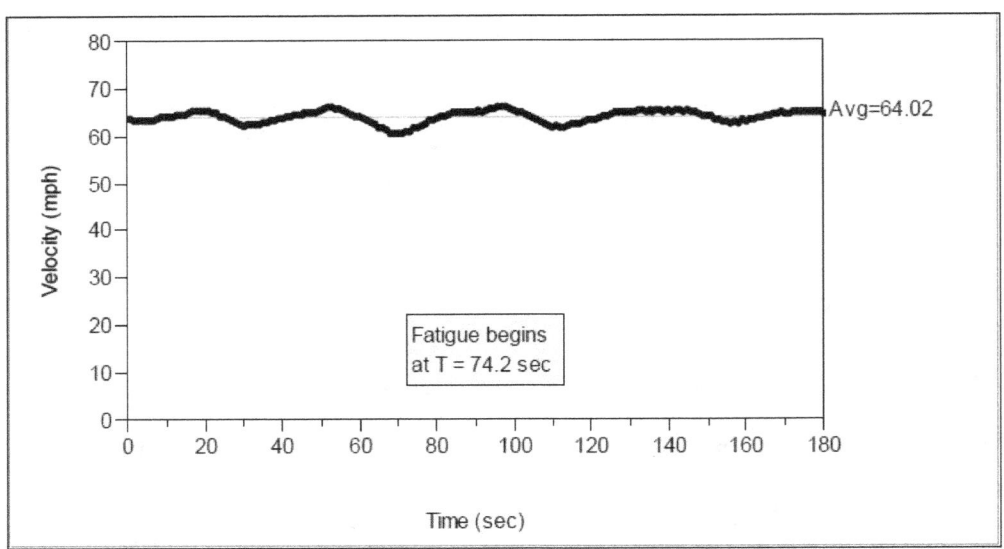

Figure 29. Individual Measurement of Velocity vs. Time (Subject 13, Event #51)

The moving range of velocity in miles per hour is shown on the vertical axis of Figure 30 as a function of time over the 180-second interval. The average value of the moving range is 0.230 mi/h. The moving-range graph looks essentially the same both before and after the driver becomes fatigued at 74.2 seconds, indicating that there is no increase in speed variation due to fatigue. Both before and after fatigue onset at 74.2 seconds, there are numerous moving range points at 0, at 0.27, and at approximately 0.56.

58

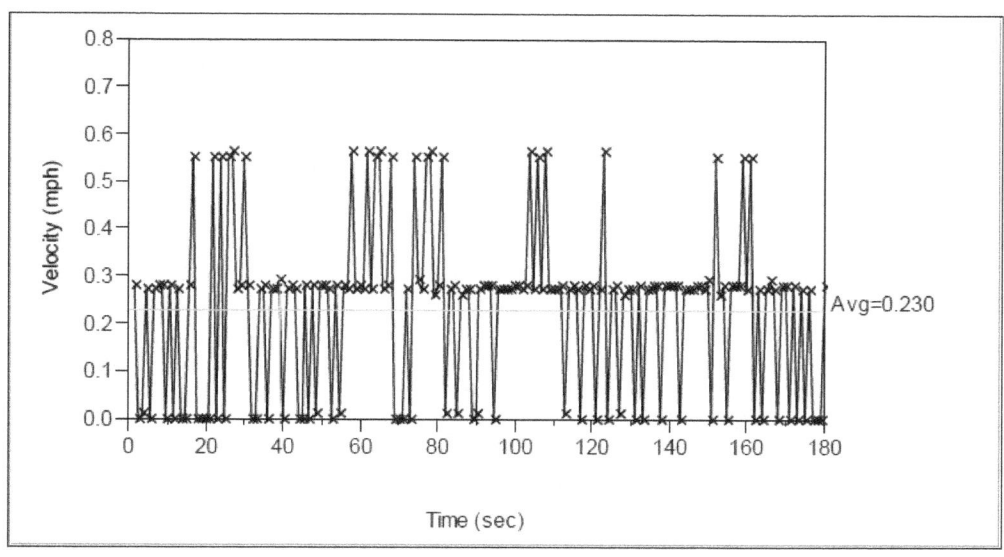

Figure 30. Moving Range of Velocity vs. Time (Subject 13, Event #51)

Figure 31 shows velocity in miles per hour on the y-axis as a function of time on the x-axis. The time scale is from 0 to 180 seconds. The velocity is a very smooth curve with velocity held steady at the overall 3-minute average of 64.47 mi/h. At approximately 20 seconds, the velocity rises slightly to about 66 mi/h, and then at 50 seconds it decreases to 63 mi/h before returning to the average value of 64.47 m/h at 105 seconds. There is a notation on the chart that the onset of fatigue occurs at 91.0 seconds.

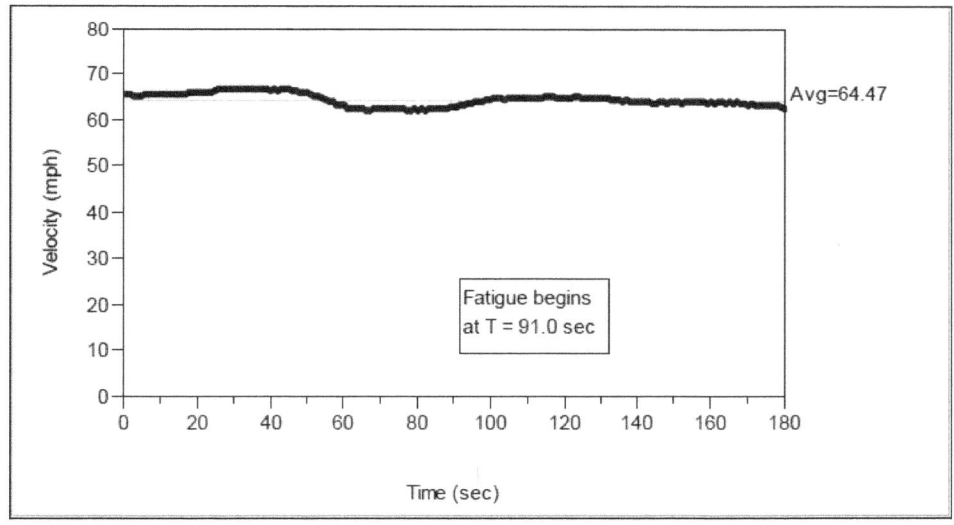

Figure 31. Individual Measurement of Velocity vs. Time (Subject 15, Event #16)

The moving range of velocity in miles per hour is shown on the vertical axis of Figure 32 as a function of time over a 180-second interval. The average value of the moving range is 0.111 mi/h. The moving-range chart looks nearly identical both before and after the onset of fatigue at 91 seconds with the exception of three values of approximately 0.56 mi/h at 60 seconds. All other values of moving range are near either 0 or 0.29 mi/h over the 3-minute interval.

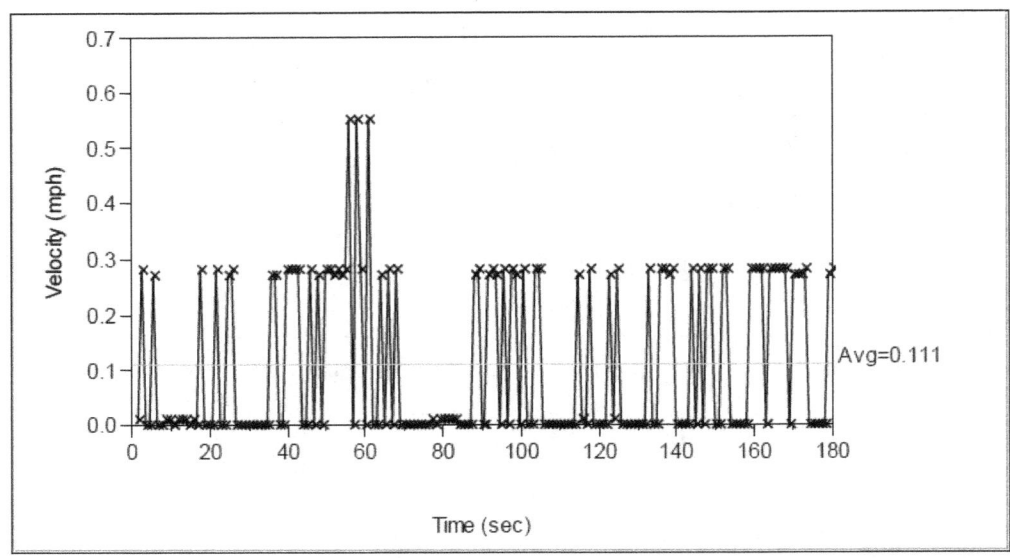

Figure 32. Moving Range of Velocity vs. Time (Subject 15, Event #16)

If drowsiness impacts a driver's ability to maintain and control vehicle speed, then one would expect to see a greater number of data points with higher moving-range values following the onset of drowsiness. Figure 25 through Figure 28 are representative of several events that showed some evidence of increased speed variability when the driver began to experience drowsiness. In both of these events, the driver was traveling at highway speeds in light traffic conditions. On the moving-range charts, it appears that more data points with higher values occur after the driver becomes drowsy. In contrast to these two examples, however, many of the events that were analyzed exhibited no apparent difference in speed variability before and after the onset of fatigue/drowsiness. This is illustrated in the events presented in Figure 29 through Figure 32. Therefore, although the analysis was somewhat limited in scope, attempts to correlate velocity variations with fatigue proved to be inconclusive. No compelling evidence was found to suggest that a driver's ability to maintain and control vehicle speed is adversely affected by fatigue and drowsiness.

3.4 RELATIONSHIP OF DRIVER DROWSINESS AND DRIVER DISTRACTION

The objective of this task was to correlate the relationship between driver drowsiness and distraction and to determine whether an L/SH driver is more or less likely to be distracted from driving when he is experiencing fatigue and drowsiness. It was also of interest to determine whether a particular distraction-related behavior is predominant during drowsiness and how this compares with periods of non-fatigued driving. Three different approaches were used to investigate the relationship of driver drowsiness and driver distraction. First of all, quantitative analyses were conducted to evaluate differences in EYETRANS and EYESOFF between periods of drowsy and alert driving. Second, a detailed video analysis of a sample of 300 events was done to compare the type and frequency of typical distraction-related activities during baseline or alert driving periods with the distraction activities observed when drivers were experiencing fatigue and drowsiness. And finally, six drivers were observed over a prolonged period (more than 30 minutes) that included drowsy and alert driving. These qualitative assessments of driver drowsiness and distraction are presented in an observational case study format. Results from these three analytical approaches are discussed in the following sections.

3.4.1 Analysis of EYETRANS and EYESOFF

Two measures of driver inattention or visual demand, EYETRANS and EYESOFF, were measured by video analysts during the detailed data reduction of 1,000 events. The definitions of these parameters are:

- EYETRANS = Number of eye transitions per minute over the 3-minute measurement interval.

- EYESOFF = Proportion of time over the 3-minute interval that the driver's eyes were off the road. This includes the time that the driver's eyes were closed or nearly closed (PERCLOS).

- EYESOFF (without drowsiness) = EYESOFF minus PERCLOS. This is a better indication of distraction or inattention since it measures only the proportion of time that the driver looked away from the road.

It can be hypothesized that drivers who make multiple short glances to gather frequent small samples of the driving environment, while devoting the largest proportion of time to the forward view, would appear to demonstrate a high level of alertness and attention to the driving task. It is also suggested that this higher level of attention would correspond to safe driving. Therefore, analyses were performed to compare EYETRANS and EYESOFF during drowsy and alert driving, and also to identify factors that may influence changes in these two measures of inattention. Note that all subsequent discussion of EYESOFF refers to the measurement of EYESOFF without drowsiness (i.e., EYESOFF minus PERCLOS).

Analysis of Variance (ANOVA) compared mean values of EYETRANS and EYESOFF for drowsy driving with baseline driving. The means are considered to be statistically significantly different if the p-value is less than 0.05. Results were obtained for all events, ORD 4 and 5 plus matching baseline events, and ORD 2 and 3 plus matching baseline events. ANOVA results are shown in Table 24.

Table 24. ANOVA Results for EYETRANS and EYESOFF

Data Stratification	Distraction Measure	Mean Fatigue	Mean Baseline	p-Value
ALL EVENTS	EYETRANS	13.89	15.44	0.0030
ALL EVENTS	EYESOFF	7.58	9.25	<0.0001
ORD 4 & 5	EYETRANS	11.90	14.60	<0.0001
ORD 4 & 5	EYESOFF	6.23	8.86	<0.0001
ORD 2 & 3	EYETRANS	15.65	17.66	0.0276
ORD 2 & 3	EYESOFF	8.78	10.31	0.0223

It can be seen that both EYETRANS and EYESOFF are higher during baseline or alert driving than during periods of fatigue and drowsiness. This suggests that drivers tend to scan the environment and check their mirrors more frequently when alert and that they may exhibit signs of "tunnel vision," or a lack of awareness of the outside driving environment, when drowsy. This may also suggest that drivers do not engage in distracting activities such as looking around at passing vehicles, tuning the radio, reading, or searching for something inside the cab when they are feeling drowsy. In addition EYETRANS and EYESOFF are lower during episodes of severe drowsiness (ORD 4 and 5) than during mild and moderate drowsy periods (ORD 2 and 3), suggesting that the tunnel vision syndrome is more pronounced when drivers experience higher levels of drowsiness.

Linear regression models using the stepwise procedure were estimated to determine the driver characteristics, environmental conditions, and roadway factors that are significantly related to driver distraction and inattention. The output from the analyses of all 1,000 events using EYETRANS and EYESOFF as dependent variables in the regression equations is shown in Table 25 and Table 26, respectively. Parameter estimates, t-ratios, and p-values for each variable are given, and the default for a variable being removed from the model is $p > 0.05$. Variables not previously defined in Section 3.2 include:

- Age = Driver's age (in years).

- TimeDuty = Time (in minutes) since the driver's shift began.

- TimeBed = Time spent in bed the previous night (in minutes).

An examination of the results in Table 25 and Table 26 leads to the following findings:

- EYETRANS and EYESOFF were both found to decrease on undivided highways (in both rural and urban areas) and in poor visibility conditions. In other words, drivers tend to focus more attention on the forward roadway when outside visibility is poor, and also when they are driving on a roadway with no physical barrier separating the directions of travel. Poor visibility and undivided roadways present a more challenging driving environment, thus increasing a driver's attention on the driving task and reducing his level of fatigue.

- The number of eye transitions away from the forward view can be expected to increase when traffic density increases, all other variables in the model being constant. This result, together with the inverse relationship of traffic density with PERCLOS that was observed previously (Table 13), confirms the belief that drivers tend to gather more frequent small samples of the environment and, as a consequence, are less susceptible to drowsiness in heavier traffic conditions.

Table 26 indicates that previous night's sleep quality rated as poor or fair decreases the proportion of time a driver's eyes are looking away from the road. Previously, we had found a positive relationship between poor/fair sleep quality and higher PERCLOS values. Thus, our analysis provides evidence that poor/fair sleep quality is a contributing factor to tunnel vision and drowsiness.

- Increases in eye transition rate and in the proportion of time a driver's eyes are off the road are associated with more experienced drivers.

- The effect of time of day on driver distraction and inattention is not as significant as its effect on driver drowsiness.

Table 25. Regression Model to Identify Factors Affecting EYETRANS (All Events; R2 = 0.166)

Variable	Parameter Estimate	t-Ratio	Prob > | t |
Intercept	10.0607	6.61	<0.0001
YrsTrucker	0.3904	5.46	<0.0001
TimeDuty	0.0039	3.64	0.0003
TimeBed	0.0089	2.27	0.0234
DENSITY	2.0929	3.53	0.0004
RURALUNDIV	-5.6318	-8.26	<0.0001
URBANUNDIV	-4.0042	-4.23	<0.0001
BADVISION	-2.4369	-3.94	<0.0001

Table 26. Regression Model to Identify Factors Affecting EYESOFF (All Events; R2 = 0.174)

Variable	Parameter Estimate	t-Ratio	Prob > | t |
Intercept	12.3955	7.59	<0.0001
Age	-0.2056	-5.45	<0.0001
YrsTrucker	0.4092	5.87	<0.0001
TimeBed	0.0076	2.66	0.0079
TIME4	0.9020	2.09	0.0373
POORSLEEP	-1.7468	-2.30	0.0217
FAIRSLEEP	-1.4127	-2.46	0.0141
RURALUNDIV	-5.0468	-10.26	<0.0001
URBANUNDIV	-2.7457	-3.97	<0.0001
BADVISION	-1.1960	-2.66	0.0079

Stepwise linear regression models were also developed for the data stratified by fatigue severity. Regression results using EYETRANS and EYESOFF as response variables are shown in Table 27 and Table 28, respectively, for ORD 4 and 5 events plus matched baseline events. For ORD 2 and 3 events, the regression models for EYETRANS and EYESOFF are provided in Table 29 and Table 30, respectively. The results of these analyses are similar to those already discussed for all 1,000 events. The major additional finding is the existence of a relationship between time of day and EYETRANS for the severe ORD 4 and 5 drowsy events, as shown in Table 27. The eye transition rate decreases significantly in the afternoon and evening. The number of eye transitions per minute is reduced by 2.9 between 12 p.m. and 3 p.m. (TIME4), by 4.4 between 3 p.m. and 6 p.m. (TIME5), and by 7.3 between 6 p.m. and 9 p.m. (TIME6), after controlling for the effects of the other variables in the model. Also, the data show that increases in EYETRANS and EYESOFF are associated with younger drivers for the less severe ORD 2 and 3 events.

Table 27. Regression Model to Identify Factors Affecting EYETRANS (ORD 4 & 5 Events; R2 = 0.249)

Variable	Parameter Estimate	t-Ratio	Prob > | t |
Intercept	11.0649	16.34	<0.0001
YrsTrucker	0.6557	5.71	<0.0001
TimeDuty	0.0122	4.28	<0.0001
TIME4	-2.9010	-2.47	0.0140
TIME5	-4.3844	-2.91	0.0037
TIME6	-7.2665	-2.43	0.0155
DENSITY	2.9650	4.05	<0.0001
RURALUNDIV	-5.9900	-7.72	<0.0001
URBANUNDIV	-4.8356	-4.03	<0.0001
BADVISION	-1.8747	-2.38	0.0177

Table 28. Regression Model to Identify Factors Affecting EYESOFF (ORD 4 & 5 Events; R2 = 0.184).

Variable	Parameter Estimate	t-Ratio	Prob > | t |
Intercept	6.6729	11.83	<0.0001
YrsTrucker	0.1865	2.62	0.0090
TIME5	-1.3676	-2.35	0.0190
DENSITY	1.1933	2.15	0.0321
RIGHTLANE	1.3560	2.60	0.0094
RURALUNDIV	-4.3874	-6.89	<0.0001
URBANUNDIV	-2.9128	-3.07	0.0023
DAYLIGHT	1.9651	3.77	0.0002

**Table 29. Regression Model to Identify Factors
Affecting EYETRANS (ORD 2 & 3 Events; R2 = 0.100)**

Variable	Parameter Estimate	t-Ratio	Prob > | t |
Intercept	24.2653	12.24	<0.0001
Age	-0.2963	-3.87	0.0001
YrsTrucker	0.5905	4.34	<0.0001
TIME5	1.8590	2.07	0.0388
RURALUNDIV	-2.7280	-2.17	0.0306
CLOUDY	-2.3639	-2.70	0.0072
BADVISION	-4.2008	-4.65	<0.0001

**Table 30. Regression Model to Identify Factors
Affecting EYESOFF (ORD 2 & 3 Events; R2 = 0.167)**

Variable	Parameter Estimate	t-Ratio	Prob > | t |
Intercept	15.4221	6.86	<0.0001
Age	-0.3512	-6.26	<0.0001
YrsTrucker	0.5221	5.33	<0.0001
TimeBed	0.0097	2.33	0.0206
RURALUNDIV	-3.4562	-3.80	0.0002
CLOUDY	-2.0083	-3.15	0.0017
BADVISION	-2.4060	-3.66	0.0003

As suggested previously, it is difficult to make cause-and-effect connections between independent and dependent measures from the results of the multiple regression analyses. For example, it cannot said that driving early in the morning causes drowsiness or that undivided highways cause an increased focus on the forward roadway. Rather, these analyses identify factors that appear to be related to driver drowsiness and driver distraction. A cautionary word must also be mentioned with regard to treating the drowsy and baseline episodes as independent events, an underlying assumption in multiple linear regression analysis. Two events sampled for the same driver on the same day may present a situation in which the two responses form a pair of measurements coming from the same experimental unit—in this case, the driver. Because the measurements are paired, treating the results as independent discards potentially useful information. Hence, while it is not incorrect to use linear regression analysis under these conditions, it should be noted that this analytical method may not have as much statistical power to signal differences in the responses as a technique that takes into account correlation between the events, like a repeated measures design. As a result, the parameter estimates of the independent variables may be biased; however, bias in the estimates will affect the magnitude of the coefficients and may not change the statistical significance. The researchers are not using the magnitude of the coefficients in a regression equation to predict values of PERCLOS, EYETRANS, and EYESOFF. Rather, they are interested only in determining which factors are significantly associated with these measures, and multiple linear regression is an appropriate analytical tool to accomplish this.

3.4.2 Analysis of 300 Events

A random sample of ORD 4 and 5 events, and matched samples of baseline (ORD 1) events, were selected to compare observed distraction activities during alert driving periods with distraction activities observed when drivers were experiencing fatigue and drowsiness. A sample of 300 events was selected from all 25 L/SH drivers who experienced severe episodes of fatigue and drowsiness. Eighty-five ORD 4 events plus 85 matched baseline events and 65 ORD 5 along with 65 matched baseline events were reviewed. Each event was 3 minutes in duration, and it should be noted that the majority (72 percent) of ORD 4 and 5 events sample also contained a period of alert, non-drowsy driving preceding the onset of drowsiness. The mean drowsiness duration for all 150 drowsy events analyzed was 118.7 seconds (standard deviation = 52.5 sec, maximum = 180 sec, minimum = 17.4 sec). The number of occurrences of each of the following secondary activities typically associated with driver distraction and drowsiness countermeasure activities were recorded:

- Reading (a delivery schedule or driving direction).
- Dialing/talking on cell phone.
- Talking to passenger.
- Tuning radio station.
- Eating and drinking.
- Smoking.

3.4.3 Drowsiness countermeasures.

Drowsiness countermeasures refer to strategies and activities that drivers undertake to counteract drowsiness, such as rubbing the face, eyes, or neck; shaking the head; stretching, squirming, or shifting around in the seat; biting the fingernails; and singing along with the radio. It should be noted that tuning the radio also includes reaching to the dashboard or instrument panel to adjust something, as well as reaching for an item inside the cab, and reading also includes looking down toward the passenger seat at something that is out of camera view. With regard to talking to a passenger, some conversations were prolonged and were considered to be a single event or occurrence; however, if an ongoing conversation was interrupted or had a gap of approximately 20 to 30 seconds, multiple occurrences of conversations were recorded.

Results from the video analysis of 300 events, showing frequency distributions of secondary activities normally associated with distraction during periods of drowsy and baseline driving, are presented in Figure 33, which is a bar graph showing the number of occurrences on the vertical axis of seven types of secondary or distraction activities (indicated on the horizontal axis) observed during the video analysis of 300 events. Two bars are shown for each distraction activity, one representing periods of fatigued driving and one representing alert or baseline driving. The numerical results are as follows:

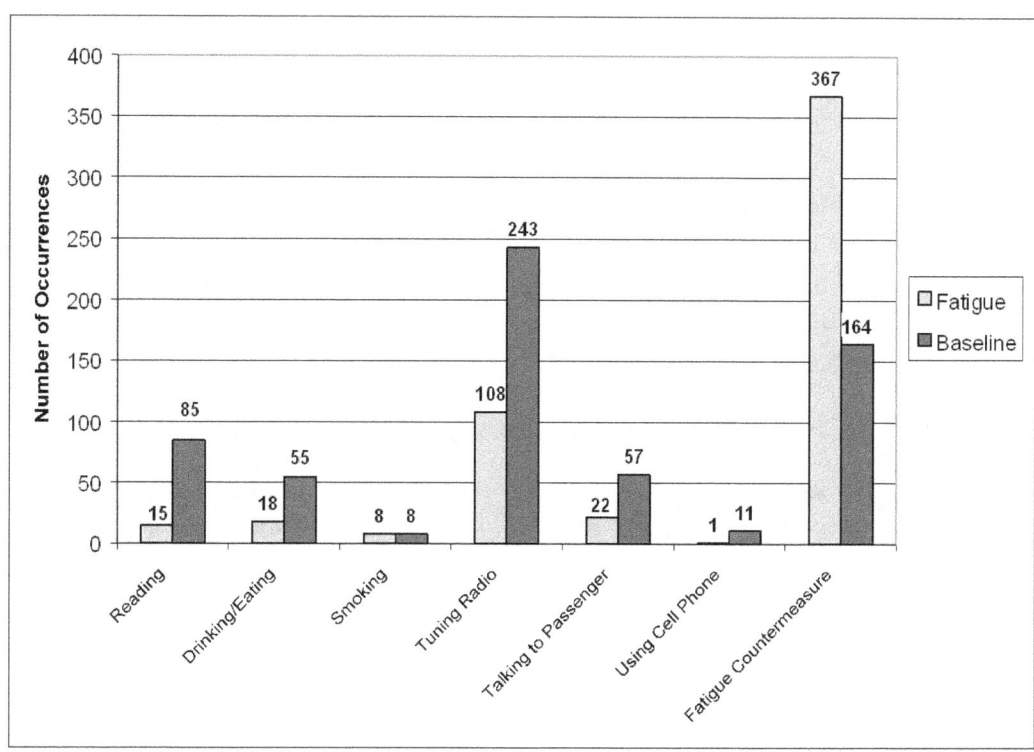

Figure 33. Distribution of Distraction Activities During Periods of Fatigued and Baseline Driving

For reading, 15 occurrences were observed during drowsy and 85 during baseline; 18 instances of eating and drinking were recorded during drowsy and 55 during baseline; for smoking, eight occurrences were observed during both drowsy and baseline driving; drivers tuned the radio station or reached toward the dashboard 108 times while drowsy and 243 times during baseline driving; 22 occurrences of talking to a passenger were observed during drowsy and 57 during baseline; one instance of cell phone usage was observed during drowsy, compared to 11 occurrences during baseline; finally, for drowsiness countermeasure activities, 367 occurrences were observed during drowsy and 164 during baseline driving.

The most commonly observed secondary activity was tuning the radio station/reaching to the dashboard. Drivers were observed to engage in this activity during periods of alert driving (n = 243) as well as when they were feeling drowsy, in an attempt to find an interesting and desirable radio station to keep them awake and alert (n = 108). In general, drivers engaged in the most "distractible" activities, such as reading a delivery schedule, using the cell phone, or eating, only during baseline or alert driving. However, taking a drink of a beverage was also occasionally used as a drowsiness countermeasure or an alerting activity to end a driver's drowsiness. It can also be seen that drivers engaged in drowsiness countermeasure activities more than twice as frequently during drowsy periods as during baseline driving.

Thus, an interesting relationship between secondary or distraction activities and driver drowsiness emerged from the review of 300 events. This relationship is illustrated in Figure 34. The figure depicts a Venn diagram in which one circle, "Fatigue," represents a typical group of activities that drivers undertake when they feel drowsy. These activities include stretching, scratching head and face, shaking head, and adjusting sitting posture. The other circle, labeled "Alert," represents a set of actions (such as reading, eating, and dialing a wireless phone) that drivers typically undertake only while alert. Where these two circles intersect there is a set of behaviors, referred to a "quasi-distraction" activities, that drivers routinely engage in when alert and awake but will also carry out when they feel drowsy, in an attempt to refresh themselves and end their fatigue. Quasi-distraction activities typically consist of drinking, smoking, talking to passengers, and tuning the radio.

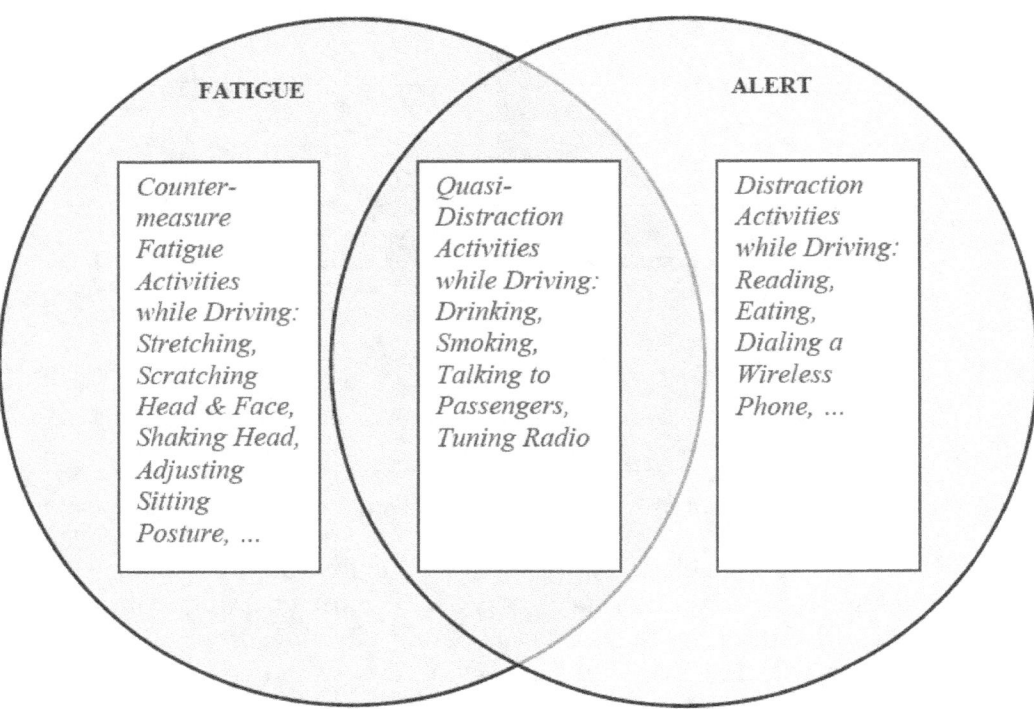

Figure 34. Relationship between Distraction Activities and Driver Fatigue

Driver workload can be thought of as a continuum with fatigue and drowsiness at one end and distraction at the other. In other words, when a driver's workload is too low, as a result of boring and monotonous driving conditions, he may tend to experience periods of drowsiness. To counteract the boredom and drowsiness, it was observed that drivers try to increase their workload by engaging in what may be considered distracting activities such as drinking a beverage, tuning the radio, talking to passengers, or (if alone) singing along with the radio, and stretching/shifting in their seats. On the other hand, when a driver is overloaded by challenging driving conditions (e.g., heavy traffic at an intersection, bad weather or visibility, or an excessively curved road) or by voluntarily introduced distraction (e.g., eating a sandwich, dialing a cell phone, or reading), his drowsiness level will be low and he will be alert and awake. Both ends of the continuum represent situations that compromise driver performance and raise serious CMV safety issues. From the analysis of naturalistic driving video data, it was observed in general that L/SH drivers did not experience severe drowsiness, nor did they willfully engage in distractible activities, when a varied and visually challenging driving environment provided them with a sufficiently demanding workload.

3.4.4 Case Studies

The relationship between driver drowsiness and driver distraction was also explored by observing drivers over a prolonged period (more than 30 minutes) before, during, and after a drowsy peak. Six drivers were selected for this qualitative analysis, and subjective observations of driver behavior during periods of drowsy and alert driving are presented below in the form of case studies. These particular six drivers were chosen because they were the subjects of a previous study of driver distraction among L/SH truck drivers that was aimed at characterizing the magnitude of the distraction problem by identifying all instances of distraction activities and also measuring their duration (Barr, Yang, Marville, Zamora, & Bey, 2001; Yang & Barr, 2002). As a result, we developed a thorough distraction "profile" for these drivers.

3.4.4.1 *Case Study #1: Subject Number 20*

This driver is 21 years of age with slightly more than 6 months of commercial driving experience. He was identified in our analysis as a "High Fatigue" driver (Fatigue Index = 10.85). A 38-minute segment of video data was reviewed before, during, and after a period of fatigue and drowsiness. The segment begins at approximately 6:10 a.m., at which time the driver had been on duty for only 40 minutes. The subject is driving on a four-lane divided highway in very light traffic. Music is playing loudly on the radio, and the driver is observed to be eating small items such as cookies or crackers. During this alert stage of driving, the driver is not very active (his eating notwithstanding) in terms of looking outside to scan the environment, checking mirrors, rubbing his face/neck, or shifting in his seat. He leaves the radio tuned to the same station, and his attention appears to be focused exclusively on the forward roadway.

A series of yawns and partial eye closures signal the onset of drowsiness. At this point, the subject is clearly aware of his drowsiness and he becomes much more "active" by engaging in a variety of drowsiness countermeasure activities. He shakes his head vigorously several times, stretches and shifts around in his seat, and sporadically sings along with the radio. He temporarily becomes alert when he checks the side-view mirror and changes from the left to the right lane to allow a vehicle approaching from the rear to pass. Traffic volume remains low and he soon falls back into drowsiness. After shaking his head a couple of more times, the driver finally pulls to the shoulder of the road. We see him "nodding off" and then he turns off the truck's engine, presumably to take a nap (the video camera stops recording when the ignition is turned off).

When the video resumes, the driver is back on the road listening to the radio. He becomes drowsy again very shortly. Once again, he shakes his head, sings to himself, and stretches in his seat, but now he begins to eat and to drink from a soda bottle to counteract his drowsiness. He continues driving on the open highway for awhile, then exits onto a signal-controlled road and turns into a shopping center to make a delivery. When he resumes driving, he is clearly awake and alert. His driving behavior is the same as before his period of drowsiness, i.e., he is relatively inactive, silent, and focused on the forward roadway with only an occasional glance out the left window. It is interesting to note that in the previous study of driver distraction (Barr et al., 2001; Yang & Barr, 2002), it was found that subject number 20 most frequently engaged in the distraction activities "singing and whistling" (47 percent of overall distraction duration; 21.5 percent of total occurrences) and "eating and drinking" (33 percent of duration; 30 percent of occurrences).

3.4.4.2   Case Study #2: Subject Number 45

This driver is a 23-year-old male with 1 year of commercial and L/SH driving experience. The Fatigue Index for this driver was 19.71, placing him near the top of the "High Fatigue" group of L/SH drivers. The 39-minute segment of videotape reviewed for this case study included a long stretch of monotonous driving on lonely, open road and included a period of extreme drowsiness on the driver's part. The segment begins at 7:15 a.m., and the driver had already been on duty for approximately 3.5 hours. The driver is proceeding on a narrow two-lane undivided rural road. Most of the traffic is moving in the opposite direction. He is engaged in sporadic conversation with a passenger who is out of camera view but who can be heard on the audio. His conversation keeps him alert, and he is attentive to the forward roadway; his glances away from the road ahead are very infrequent.

When the crowsy period begins, he is driving on a three-lane road (two lanes in his direction of travel, since he is ascending a hill) on which other vehicles are few and far between. Conversation with his passenger ends and his eyelids grow very heavy. Throughout his drowsiness, he is scratching his head and smoothing his hair. These periods of extreme drowsiness are temporarily and briefly interrupted at times when he begins talking with his passenger again; thus, conversation seems to be the most common and most effective alerting activity and drowsiness countermeasure.

During his period of drowsy driving, this subject occasionally crosses over the double-yellow centerline into the opposing lane. However, it must also be noted that he exhibits the same driving behavior when alert and attentive. In other words, cutting curves and using both lanes on a curved roadway in the absence of approaching traffic seems to be typical driving behavior for this driver whether or not he is in a state of drowsiness. The driver is aware of his drowsiness and sleepiness, and at one point comments to his passenger that "this is such a long and boring drive" and "you're going to have to sing to me or something . . . to keep me alive." He bounces in his seat, rubs his face, and talks to the passenger to counteract the drowsiness and monotony. Again, his eyes are fixed mostly straight ahead.

This driver is all over the road when he is severely drowsy. He somehow manages to stay in his own lane when other vehicles approach in the opposite lane. Results from the previous study of L/SH driver distraction (Barr et al., 2001; Yang & Barr, 2002) indicated that this driver's behavior was characterized primarily by long conversations with his passenger. Of his 21 total hours of recorded driving time, this man spent 17.2 hours (82 percent) engaged in conversation with his passenger. Therefore, conversation is his primary distraction, but, in his case, it is a "good" distraction that promotes safety by keeping him alert. In the post- drowsiness period, the driver is following a car that, in his opinion, is going too slowly. He complains repeatedly about it, but at least his irritation keeps him awake and attentive.

3.4.4.3   Case Study #3: Subject Number 15

This driver is 28 years of age and has been driving an L/SH truck for 4 years. He is also in the "High Fatigue" group of drivers as determined by his calculated Fatigue Index of 12.2. A 34-minute video segment begins with the driver alert and attentive at about 5 p.m. He is driving in fairly heavy afternoon-rush-hour traffic, but soon turns onto a four-lane divided highway with moderate traffic. He is continuously scanning the surrounding environment, and he is listening to the radio but not "channel-surfing." He proceeds onto lightly traveled rural roads—first a two-lane road, and then a four-lane road—and begins to experience a series of drowsy episodes. While he is drowsy, his glances to the mirrors and out the driver-side window are significantly reduced. We then see the driver perk up and light a cigarette to offset his drowsiness. He also turns up the volume on the radio, but he again lapses into drowsiness. Smoking temporarily relieves his drowsiness; however, he is driving on a very lonely stretch of road and still appears to be drowsy. When the distraction behavior of this driver was studied (Barr et al., 2001), it was discovered that his most frequent distraction activity, by a large margin, was the relatively benign activity of scratching his face and hair (58 percent of overall occurrences, but only 7.5 percent of total distraction duration). This behavior was not particularly evident during the 34-minute segment reviewed for this case study. The distraction study also identified this driver as a smoker, and it was found that "eating/drinking/smoking" was the distraction event in which he engaged for the longest duration (58 percent of total distraction duration).

This driver's drowsiness is manifested in heavy eyelids and slow eye closings. During these periods he does nothing to counteract the drowsiness by stretching or shifting in his seat, shaking his head, or rubbing his face. His eyes are generally focused only on the road ahead, thus exhibiting some tunnel vision. He becomes alert and resumes his more frequent glances out the windows when he turns off the highway and arrives at his destination at the end of his shift. At this point, he has been on duty for more than 9.5 hours.

3.4.4.4 Case Study #4: Subject Number 19

Driver number 19 is 19 years old and has worked as an L/SH truck driver for 8 months. The earlier analysis placed him in the "High Fatigue" group of drivers (Fatigue Index = 11.61). The 38-minute driving segment begins at approximately 6:45 a.m. on a two-lane undivided rural road just 10 minutes after the beginning of his work shift. He soon turns onto a four-lane rural divided highway; traffic is very light. The driver is listening to the radio, and prior to the onset of fatigue he repeatedly glances down at the radio and changes the station to find something he likes. Even as he begins to show signs of drowsiness (i.e., frequent slow eye blinks, yawns, and some eye closings), he continues changing radio stations. It should be noted that tuning the radio was a common distraction activity identified by analysts for this driver in the previous study of driver distraction; 17 percent of all the instances of distraction-related events involved tuning the radio.

When this driver is feeling fatigued and drowsy, he is focused on the road ahead with only an occasional glance out his side window. He tries to counteract the drowsiness by rubbing his eyes and opening his eyes wide. During a brief interlude between drowsy episodes, he picks up an order form or delivery schedule and reads it and also writes on it as he drives. He continues to channel-surf on the radio. He also drinks a beverage between drowsy episodes in an attempt to stay awake and alert. In addition, this driver has a habit of biting his fingernails for long periods of time; he does this mostly while alert, but also between drowsy events.

This driver was observed to engage in distracting activities such as reading an order form, drinking a soda, and changing radio stations prior to the onset of drowsiness and also between drowsy spells. During drowsiness, he primarily engages in drowsiness countermeasure activities such as stretching in his seat, rubbing his eyes and neck, and biting his nails. After his drowsiness peak, he is not distracted (i.e., by reading or drinking), but he keeps his fingers in his mouth, biting his nails for nearly the entire 10-minute post- drowsiness period.

3.4.4.5   Case Study #5: Subject Number 24

This driver is 28 years of age and has been employed as a commercial truck driver for only 2 months. His calculated Fatigue Index of 12.8 places him in the "High Fatigue" group of drivers. A 32-minute segment of driving data begins at about 3 p.m., at which time the driver had been on duty for 8 hours and 40 minutes. He is driving on a two-lane undivided road with fairly light traffic, and he is engaged in conversation with a passenger in the truck. He then merges onto a four-lane divided highway with very light traffic, still talking to his passenger. The driver does not appear to be distracted while talking to the passenger (although it should be noted that cognitive distraction cannot be determined by analyzing naturalistic driving data); he is attentive to the driving task, checks mirrors frequently, and continuously scans the outside environment. The previous study of driver distraction cited "talking to passenger" as the predominant distraction activity for this driver (Barr et al., 2001); 59 percent of the overall time spent engaged in distracting activities was spent in conversation with his passenger. Other common distractions included talking on a cell phone (7.6 percent of total distraction duration), singing or whistling (4.3 percent), and eating/drinking (17 percent).

The driving conditions are very monotonous—clear weather and lonely, open highway—and the driver gradually shows signs of increasing drowsiness. He wards it off by talking to his passenger; both the duration and the severity of drowsy events appear to be reduced by engaging in conversation. Several instances were observed in which the driver was simultaneously yawning and talking. The frequency of his glances to the mirrors and outside the truck decreases when he is feeling drowsy and fatigued.

The driver eventually encounters heavier traffic, at which point he becomes alert and attentive, although not involved in a conversation with his passenger. During this period of alert and silent driving, he is continually glancing to both sides, looking outside and checking the side-view mirrors.

3.4.4.6   Case Study #6: Subject Number 46

This driver is 39 years old and has 2 years of commercial and L/SH driving experience. He was categorized as a "Low Fatigue" driver, based on his calculated Fatigue Index of 4.44. This driver was observed for 31 minutes before, during, and after a period in which he suffers several minor episodes of drowsiness. The segment begins at 6:45 a.m., approximately 45 minutes after starting his shift. He is driving on a rural undivided highway in very light traffic, and he is chewing gum and listening to the radio. Prior to the onset of drowsiness and during his period of drowsy driving, the driver rarely glances at his mirrors or outside the side windows. He keeps his eyes focused on the forward roadway. In addition, the driver bites his fingernails fairly regularly; this behavior appears to be more habitual than as a countermeasure to alleviate drowsiness. This is consistent with the results obtained from this driver in the distraction study, in which it was found that more than half his distraction activities involved scratching or rubbing his face or head, biting his fingernails, and grooming. In terms of overall time spent being distracted, eating, drinking, and smoking accounted for about 65 percent of his overall distraction duration. He was not, however, seen eating or drinking or smoking a cigarette during the 31-minute segment that was reviewed.

When the drowsy peak ends, the driver appears to be more aware of the outside environment. He is driving on a four-lane divided highway in light traffic. He glances out his side windows occasionally, but not frequently, and he is also "distracted" by a car passing on his left. He continues to bite his nails for long periods of time, and he is chewing gum throughout the entire segment (both while drowsy and while alert); thus chewing gum does not prevent drowsiness.

In general, this driver is much more active following his period of drowsiness. He is not distracted, but he is considerably more animated than the periods before and during drowsiness in terms of glancing around, shifting in his seat, scratching and rubbing his face, and chewing his fingernails. The driving conditions become more varied during this time as he transitions from one highway to another several times, and he also stops once at a delivery destination.

In summary, the six drivers observed in the case studies were generally found to be more attentive to the surrounding environment while alert. During these periods, drivers tended to glance outside and check the mirrors more frequently to obtain small samples of the external driving conditions. When fatigued, drivers focused on the forward roadway, and as a whole, they engaged more frequently in activities such as rubbing their faces or necks and singing with the radio to counteract the effects of drowsiness.

4. CONCLUSIONS

Naturalistic driving data are a valuable source of information for exploring driving behaviors and human factors issues such as drowsiness and driver distraction. The researchers conducted a study to characterize episodes of driver fatigue and drowsiness and to assess the impact of driver drowsiness on driving performance by analyzing approximately 900 hours of continuous video data of local/short-haul (L/SH) truck drivers. In this study, all instances of driver drowsiness were identified, and relationships between driver drowsiness and operational/external factors, driver performance, and driver distraction were investigated. Predictive models were developed to determine the driver characteristics (such as age, years of commercial driving experience, sleep quality/quantity) and external or environmental factors (such as time of day, weather, traffic density) that influence the likelihood of driver fatigue and drowsiness occurring on the job.

Several analytical techniques, including analysis of variance, contingency table analysis, multiple linear regression, and logistic regression, were applied to the data obtained from the detailed reduction of the L/SH video data. Generally, these methodologies produced consistent results. One of the major findings of this study was that every analysis provided evidence of a strong association between drowsiness and time of day. The early-morning time period between 6 a.m. and 9 a.m. was especially problematic for the L/SH drivers. Logistic regression results showed that drowsiness was twice as likely to occur between 6 a.m. and 9 a.m., as compared to baseline, and a linear regression model indicated a significant relationship between this time period and an increase in drowsiness as measured by PERCLOS. Conversely, a decrease in PERCLOS (i.e., increased alertness) was associated with the time period between 12 p.m. and 3 p.m. These results, together with the finding that approximately 30 percent of all observed instances of drowsiness occurred within the first hour of the work shift, suggest that drivers may not be fully refreshed and awake when they begin their workday. Similar results showing a strong and consistent relationship between driver alertness and time of day were also found in other research studies (Wylie et al., 1996b; Dingus et al., 2002).

Drowsiness was also found to be associated with younger and less experienced drivers. Odds ratios estimated using logistic regression indicated that drivers in the 19–25-year-old age group were nine times more likely to be classified in the "High Fatigue" group than older drivers. Similarly, inexperienced drivers with less than 1 year of commercial driving experience were about seven times more likely to be "High Fatigue" drivers than were those with more driving experience. In addition, a somewhat weak association between sleep quantity/quality and drowsy driving was established in this study. Analysis of variance results showed a significantly lower average sleep duration, as measured by Actiwatch data, on the nights preceding fatigue or drowsy events compared to baseline events. And drivers' self-reported subjective assessments of sleep quality were significantly related to increases in PERCLOS in linear regression models; that is, poor sleep quality can be expected to increased PERCLOS, all else being equal. The absence of a stronger link between sleep behavior and driver fatigue can most likely be attributed to the nature of the sleep data obtained during the L/SH field test. Due to the unreliability of the Actiwatch wrist monitor, usable information about actual sleep duration was lost for several of the L/SH drivers. Also, time spent in bed, a surrogate measure of sleep quantity, turned out to be a poor predictor of driver drowsiness.

Although the analysis of the relationship between driver characteristics and drowsiness produced some interesting results with important implications for driver fitness and safety performance, it also highlighted a limitation in the existing data set. Developing a demographic profile of a person most likely to experience on-the-job drowsiness was difficult since the list of driver characteristics used as independent variables in a mathematical model to classify drivers according to their propensity for drowsiness was somewhat limited. Gathering more information about a driver's physiology (e.g., body mass index), medical history, and current use of medications, as well as complete and accurate data on sleep quantity and quality, may prove useful in identifying at-risk drivers.

This study provided a better understanding of the relationship between driver drowsiness and driver distraction and inattention. Quantitative evidence was obtained to verify the hypothesis that drivers suffering from fatigue and drowsiness experience "tunnel vision." When a driver becomes drowsy, the rate of eye transitions and the proportion of time his eyes are off the forward roadway were both found to decrease. Therefore, a drowsy driver is less aware of the driving environment around him, and his ability to recognize potential hazards from other vehicles or objects outside the vehicle is compromised. This study also found that driving conditions such as poor visibility and undivided highways tend to increase the driver's focus on the forward roadway.

Observation of driver behavior from the continuous video data revealed that in the majority of cases, drowsiness occurred during periods of extremely low driver workload brought on by boredom and monotony. In these cases, the driver would often respond by engaging in secondary activities typically associated with driver distraction or drowsiness countermeasure activities, in an effort to increase his workload. Drowsiness countermeasures such as rubbing the face and neck, stretching and shifting in the seat, and singing along with the radio were observed much more frequently during periods of drowsiness than during alert driving. On the other hand, secondary activities that demand a great deal of driver attention, such as eating, reading, and using a wireless phone, occurred predominantly when the driver was awake and alert. Drivers must continually allocate attention to competing tasks, both driving and non-driving. This study provided some interesting insights into how drivers handle competing tasks and how they respond to situations when they feel drowsy and fatigued. Still, few quantitative data exist to characterize the relationship between driver workload, distraction, and drowsiness. Providing a better understanding of this relationship could be an area for further research.

Two measures of driver performance, lane-keeping and speed management, were evaluated in an effort to correlate driver fatigue and performance. Because lane-tracking sensors were not included in the onboard instrumentation system in the L/SH field study, investigation of a driver's lane-keeping performance was limited to observational analysis of video data. Gross violations and obvious lane excursions were apparent in the video data, but variations in vehicle position within the lane and minor lane drifting were not easily detectable. A driver's ability to maintain lane position is adversely affected by fatigue and drowsiness. This presents a traffic safety concern, as evidenced by the fact that, according to General Estimates System (GES) crash data, approximately three of every four crashes in which fatigue/sleepiness is cited as a contributing factor are single-vehicle roadway-departure crashes. Thus, lane-tracking instrumentation should be standard equipment in all future naturalistic driving field studies. The results of an analysis of speed variations during periods of drowsy driving were inconclusive. No compelling evidence was found in this study to suggest that a driver's ability to maintain and control vehicle speed is severely affected by fatigue and drowsiness.

This study provided an analytical framework for quantitatively assessing driver fatigue and drowsiness as a function of driver characteristics and the driving environment. It is recommended that this work be the basis for a follow-on study to develop a more robust and comprehensive predictor of drowsiness using a combination of physiological data (PERCLOS) with other driver and vehicle performance data (e.g., lane-keeping, speed variation, time-to-collision). Current drowsy-driver warning systems incorporate PERCLOS as the primary measure of drowsiness. However, the PERCLOS monitor has some operational limitations and deficiencies; for example, it does not work reliably in daylight, or for drivers who wear eyeglasses. Therefore, it becomes important to consider what other indicators could be used to warn a driver that he is becoming drowsy when the PERCLOS drowsiness monitor is not available or is not performing reliably. A future investigation is recommended to set up equations to predict PERCLOS on the basis of performance measures such as lane position, speed variation, and relative position to forward vehicles, and to develop an algorithm that incorporates physiological data as well as vehicle/driver performance data into a drowsy-driver warning system.

REFERENCES

Abrams, C., Shultz T., & Wylie, C. (1997). *Commercial Motor Vehicle Driver Fatigue, Alertness, and Countermeasures Survey.* Report No. FHWA-MC-99-067. Federal Highway Administration, Office of Motor Carriers, U.S. Department of Transportation.

Balkin, T., Thome D., Sing H., Thomas M., Redmond, D. Wesensten, N., et al. (2000). *Effects of Sleep Schedules on Commercial Motor Vehicle Driver Performance.* Report No. DOT-MC-00-133. Federal Motor Carrier Safety Administration, U.S. Department of Transportation.

Barr, L., Yang, C. Y. D., Marville, R., Zamora, A., & Bey, S. (2001). Analysis of Naturalistic Driving Behaviors of Truck Drivers, Phase I Results: Driver Distraction Analysis of Local/Short Haul Naturalistic Data. Project Memorandum DOT-VNTSC-HS137-PM-00-01. Volpe National Transportation Systems Center, U.S. Department of Transportation.

Dingus, T. A., Neale, V. L., Garness, S. A., Hanowski, R. J., Kiesler, A. S., Lee, S. E., et al. (2002). *Impact of Sleeper Berth Usage on Driver Fatigue: Final Project Report.* Contract No. DTFH61-96-00068. Federal Motor Carrier Safety Administration, U.S. Department of Transportation.

Hanowski, R. J., Wierwille, W. W., Garness, S. A., & Dingus, T. A. (2000). *Impact of Local/Short Haul Operations on Driver Fatigue.* Report No. DOT-MC-00-203. Federal Motor Carrier Safety Administration, U.S. Department of Transportation.

Hanowski, R. J., Wierwille, W. W., Gellatly, A. W., Early, N., & Dingus, T. A. (1998). *Impact of Local/Short Haul Operations on Driver Fatigue: Task 1 Report—Focus Group Summary and Analysis.* Report No. FHWA-MC-98029. Federal Highway Administration, Office of Motor Carriers, U.S. Department of Transportation.

Massie, D. L., Blower, D., & Campbell, K. L. (1998). *Local/Short Haul Fatigue Crash Data Analysis.* Report No. FHWA-MC-98-016. Federal Highway Administration, Office of Motor Carriers, U.S. Department of Transportation.

O'Neill, T. R., Krueger, G. P., Van Hemel, S. B., & McGowan, A. L. (1999). *Effects of Operating Practices on Commercial Driver Alertness.* Report No. FHWA-MC-99-140. Federal Highway Administration, Office of Motor Carriers, U.S. Department of Transportation.

Stutts, J. C., Wilkins, J. W., & Vaughn, B. V. (1999). *Why Do People Have Drowsy Driver Crashes? Input from Drivers Who Just Did.* Final Report, AAA Foundation for Traffic Safety.

Wierwille, W. W. & Ellsworth L. A. (1994). Evaluation of Driver Drowsiness by Trained Raters. *Accident Analysis and Prevention, Vol. 26,* No. 5, pp. 571–581.

Wierwille, W. W. (1999). Historical Perspective on Slow Eyelid Closure: Whence PERCLOS? *Ocular Measures of Driver Alertness, Technical Conference Proceedings,* pp. 31–52. Transportation Safety Associates.

Wylie, C. D., Shultz, T., Miller, J. C., Mitler, M. M., & Mackie, R. R. (1996a). *Commercial Motor Vehicle Driver Fatigue and Alertness Study: Technical Summary.* Report No. FHWA-MC-97-001. Federal Highway Administration, Office of Motor Carriers, U.S. Department of Transportation.

Wylie, C. D., Shultz, T., Miller, J. C., Mitler, M. M., & Mackie, R. R. (1996b). *Commercial Motor Vehicle Driver Fatigue and Alertness Study: Final Report.* Report No. FHWA-MC-97-002. Federal Highway Administration, Office of Motor Carriers, U.S. Department of Transportation.

Yang, C. Y. D. & Barr L. C. (2002). Analysis of Naturalistic Driving Behaviors of Truck Drivers, Phase II Results: Eye Glance Behavior and Driving Performance during Distracting Events. Project Memorandum DOT-VNTSC-NHTSA-02-06. Volpe National Transportation Systems Center, U.S. Department of Transportation.